CASH FLOW CONTROL

CASH FLOW CONTROL

Brian Coyle

CIB PUBLISHING

FINANCIAL
EDUCATION

CIB Publishing
c/o The Chartered Institute of Bankers
Emmanuel House
4-9 Burgate Lane
Canterbury
Kent
CT1 2XJ
United Kingdom

Telephone: 01227 762600

CIB Publishing publications are published by The Chartered Institute of Bankers, a non-profit making registered educational charity.

Typeset by The Foundry
Printed by WBC Book Manufacturers, Bridgend

ISBN 0-85297-447-7

Contents

Introduction to Cash Flow Control

A control is a check or restraint. Controls are associated with methods or instruments for keeping events within acceptable limits and for directing events towards a desired outcome. Cash flow control, therefore, is a technique used to regulate the flow of cash receipts into a business, cash transfers between different parts of the business and cash payments by the business.

The Need for Cash Flow Control

The objectives of treasury management are mainly concerned with funding, liquidity and risk management in order

- to ensure that funds are available to support the company's desired scale of operations
- to maintain adequate liquidity
- to keep credit risk, foreign currency risk and interest rate risk within acceptable limits
- to contribute towards company profits from investment of surplus cash.

All these have cash flow implications.

Cash flow is crucial for businesses. A company must have access to cash to make payments for goods and services, simply to stay in business. Although money can be obtained from external funding sources, such as shareholders and banks, the main source of cash either will be trading activities or, in the case of financial companies, loans and investments. In the long term, cash received from trading or investments and loans must exceed operational cash payments for a company to survive. An operating cash surplus is a key indicator of a viable business.

Cash flow also affects a company's liquidity. Liquidity describes cash-in-hand and convertibility of assets into cash. A company is liquid if it has sufficient cash, or has assets that will be or could be converted into cash in the near future, in order to meet its payment obligations. It also could be argued that a company is liquid if it has ready access to cash from external sources, such as a bank-borrowing facility.

A lack of liquidity, whether episodic or chronic, implies an inability to meet payment obligations when they fall due. Payments might have to be postponed, or emergency measures taken such as borrowing or raising extra share capital to pay outstanding debts or disposing of certain assets (asset disposals). A liquidity shortage might be temporary, but if it continues in the long term, sources of funding such as interbank facilities could evaporate, pushing the company into insolvency. Indeed, liquidity problems are the leading cause of small and medium-sized enterprises (SMEs) bankruptcies despite the fact that many of these entities are viable concerns.

Ready access to cash also gives a company the financial flexibility to take expenditure decisions if and whenever it wishes, without the constraint of having to seek new funding. Healthy cash flows and large cash balances can put a company into a strong position, to launch a takeover bid or invest in a new venture for example, without the need for approval from shareholders or bankers.

When trading profits yield a higher return than cash on deposit, cash-rich companies with a relatively weak trading position could become vulnerable to a takeover bid. It is also arguable that if a trading company has a large and long-term cash surplus, it should pay out the excess cash as dividends to shareholders or in the form of share buy-backs. Trading companies are in business to trade, not to invest cash, although directors who believe in a large cash surplus as a war chest for potential takeover bids would disagree with this view.

Because healthy cash flows are vital for business, there should be a system for cash flow control by management. In a very small business, the proprietor-manager can exercise full personal control over cash. In large companies, particularly multinationals, control cannot be effective without formal organization.

Targets for Cash Flow Control

Cash flow control management applies to cash flows from operations, funding activities and investment activities.

- Cash flows from trading operations should be in surplus.
- Investment in working capital should not be excessive.
- Surplus cash balances should be invested.
- Long-term investment and funding plans should be consistent with the company's ability to generate cash from trading operations.
- Cash flows within an international or multinational company could be organized to reduce exposures to currency risk.

Achieving Cash Flow Control

The essential ingredients for cash flow control in all but the smallest of companies are

- organization
- information
- planning and policies.

Organization is needed to allocate authority and responsibilities for cash management, at local, national and multinational levels.

Information about cash flows and cash balances is necessary to prompt management into action. Each company's management will have its own views about what information should be provided, and who should receive it. The general observation can be applied that unless a manager receives information about cash or cash flows, he or she will feel no responsibility for cash and under no obligation to monitor cash flows.

Controls must be directed towards a plan or target. Managers can judge the need for control action only if actual results are diverging from their desired course. Cash flow targets could be formulated within a plan or budget, and as policies or rules and regulations, for example for credit terms, sales discounts, authorizing expenditures. Periodic reviews of cash management also could reveal whether there is inefficiency and poor cash flow regulation.

These issues are further explored in some detail here.

Organizing for Cash Flow Control

Cash management, including cash flow control, must have an organizational framework that clearly defines who is to be responsible for

- collecting cash
- authorizing payments
- making payments
- bank accounts and transferring funds between accounts
- arranging overdraft facilities and loans
- investing cash surpluses
- foreign currency transactions.

In a small company, the problem can be to make sure that someone actually does the job. It is all too easy for a busy finance director or chief accountant to overlook the consequences of not chasing customers for prompt payment, delays in banking cash receipts, and failure to use cash surpluses with maximum efficiency.

In larger companies, the problem can be to establish a framework of authority and responsibility for individuals and departments.

A Framework of Responsibilities

Someone should be responsible for every aspect of cash management, and there should be no areas of uncertainty where no one is willing to accept responsibility. Nor should there be scope for disputes over who has the authority for certain areas of cash management.

Example
Sierra is a large European-based company that centralizes responsibility for banking receipts and making payments in the financial controller's department of its head office. The managers of operating divisions in the company can sanction spending up to a specified limit. Suppliers send invoices to the operating division managers, who authorize the invoices and send them to the financial controller for payment.

Analysis
Authority to spend and the responsibility for making payments are clearly defined. However, a potential area for disagreement is deciding *when* payments should be made. Operational managers might agree credit terms with suppliers, and instruct the financial controller to pay promptly in accordance with these terms. The financial controller, on the other hand, might claim the right to delay payments beyond the due date in order to preserve cash balances and avoid borrowing on overdraft to make the payments. Unless it is clearly specified who is allowed to decide when payments should be made, there is scope for dispute.

In allocating authority and responsibility for cash management, it is useful to distinguish between operational cash flows and cash flows for financing and investing activities.

Operational Cash Flows

Operational cash flows are receipts and payments for trading activities. The allocation of responsibilities for these cash flows varies between companies according to size, management structure, geographical spread and where the point of contact exists between the company and its suppliers and customers.

In a fully decentralized organization, such as a diversified group with subsidiaries trading under different names and in different markets, each subsidiary or business unit can have its own bank account, with full responsibility for its own invoicing, receivables and payables.

In partially decentralized companies each business unit or subsidiary could deal with invoicing and cash receipts, but head office might handle all payments.

In a centralized organization, all invoicing, receivables and payables would be a head-office responsibility.

To establish a framework of cash management responsibility, a number of questions should be addressed.

- Can head office instruct business units to transfer cash from their bank account to a head office account?
- Can head office instruct a business unit to change the bank that it uses?
- Who should make cash payments, head office or the business units themselves?
- Can head office refuse to make a payment that has been requested by a business unit?
- Can a business unit arrange its own local funding, or must all funding be managed through head office?

Example 1
One such framework for cash management is illustrated in the diagram on the page opposite.

Partially Decentralized Cash Responsibilities

1. Head Office Responsible for All Payments and Cash Balances

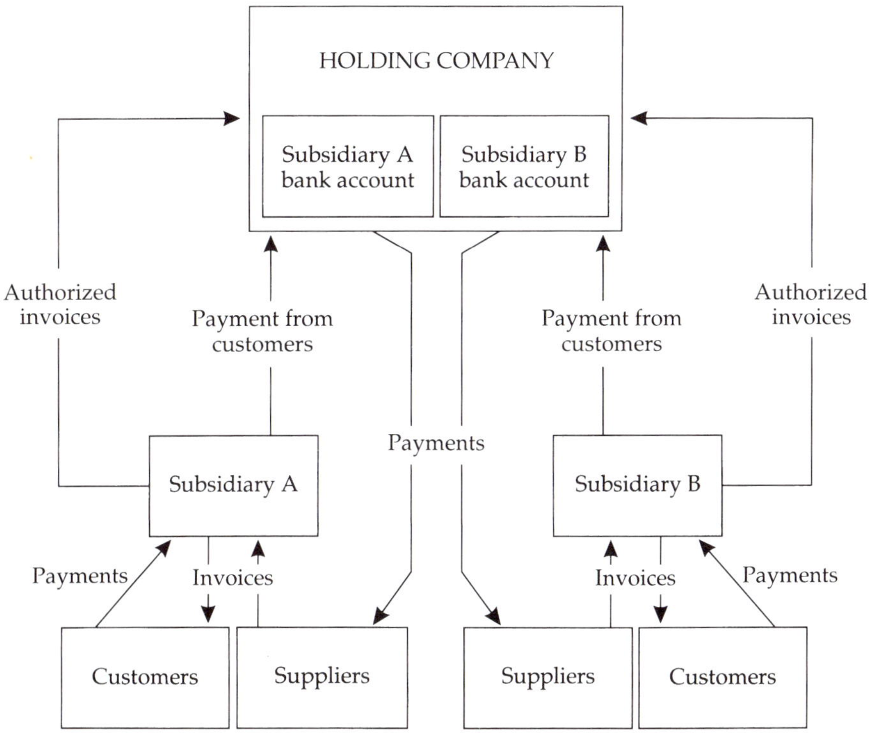

Partially Decentralized Cash Responsibilities
2. Head Office Responsible for Large Payments and Surplus Cash Balances

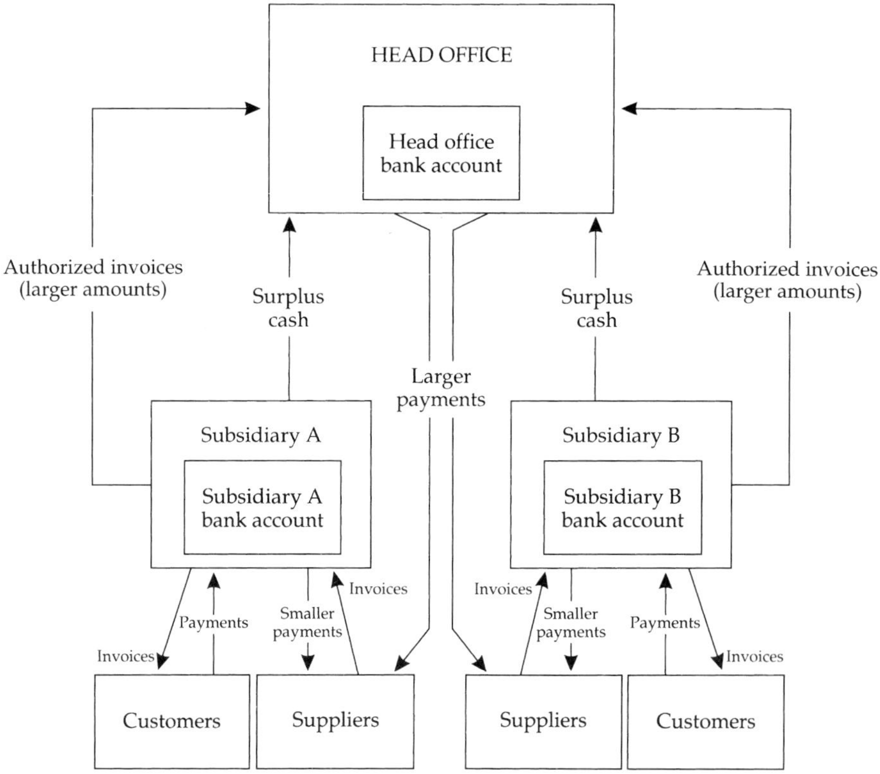

In this arrangement, there is a bank account for each subsidiary under the control of head office. Each subsidiary invoices its customers and banks the payments received. The authority to make payments from its account, however, is restricted to head office management, for example the group finance director and financial controller. Suppliers will send invoices to the subsidiary, where the payment is authorized. The authorized invoice is then remitted to head office that makes the payment from its subsidiary's account. Responsibility for cash flow therefore is shared, with the subsidiary's management responsible for receipts and head office responsible for payments.

Example 2
An alternative framework is to allow each subsidiary or business unit to make payments from its own bank account, up to a specified spending limit. Receipts from customers are lodged in the subsidiary's own bank account, but surplus cash balances are transferred to a head office bank account from which large payments are made.

In the example shown previously, the subsidiaries' managements have responsibility for receipts and some payments, but head office has control over large expenditures.

Allocating responsibilities for operational receipts and payments has implications for control. The control of cash flows should be the responsibility of managers who are authorized to collect receipts and make payments. In a centralized organization, cash flow responsibilities will rest with head office. In a decentralized organization, local management will be responsible for day-to-day operational cash flow control, although a head office treasury unit or finance department should exercise a supervisory control function.

Financing and Investment Cash Flows

Control over cash flows for investments and financing also can be shared between head office and local business units, particularly when the business units are located in different countries. However, some responsibilities must be the prerogative of head office, such as raising share capital, long-term loans, capital gearing, acquisitions and major capital expenditures.

Central Treasury Department

A central treasury, where one exists in a large group of companies, should not be involved with day-to-day cash flow control. Local payments, invoicing, collections and customer credit decisions should be the responsibility of the local financial controller. Central treasury involvement would be appropriate, however, for policy formation in these areas, and for overall cash flow and liquidity management within the group.

A central unit is in a position to monitor developments in tax and regulatory conditions as well as banking facilities, particularly in other countries. It could also recommend improvements that could be made, particularly in cross-border and multi-currency cash management.

Banking Arrangements

Banking arrangements are described more fully in *Cash Collection and Transmission,* another title in this series. However, they are also relevant to cash-flow control.

It is extremely important to establish a good relationship with one bank, and possibly two, for cash handling and money transfer activities. Once a bank has been selected and a relationship established, a company should consider changing banks only if

- it is getting poor service from its branch; for example, if the company believes that check-clearing times should be faster
- the bank is unable to provide either enough services or services of a sufficient quality or sophistication
- bank charges seem too high. In today's competitive banking environment, this should not be the case
- it can achieve cleared funds more quickly.

Multinational companies might want bank accounts in several countries. Although implementation of the euro is expected to consolidate and simplify banking relations and foreign exchange management in an intra-European context, it will also make it possible for companies to find more competitive offers. The final choice of bank will depend partly on the local services provided by that bank, and partly on the services the bank provides for cross-border money transfers and balance reporting to head office.

The ability of a group to organize multi-currency banking arrangements will continue to be a topic of concern for the global multinational.

Within the euro zone such arrangements are expected to change significantly with regard to pricing, invoicing and netting arrangements. The ability of the group to manage these arrangements also can be limited by a number of factors. For example, if some subsidiaries were to be only partly owned, this could affect the group's ability to switch cash balances through inter-subsidiary loans or through dividend payments to head office.

Companies with several bank accounts might wish to control their combined cash balances, or payments between the accounts. Two such arrangements are pooling and netting.

Pooling

Pooling is an arrangement whereby the cash balances in several different bank accounts of the company or group are pooled together into a single account known as a cash pool.

Example

Omega has five bank accounts. The balances on these accounts at the end of a day are as follows:

Account Number	**Balance**	
	$	
1	20,000	credit
2	35,000	credit
3	25,000	debit (overdrawn)
4	5,000	credit
5	10,000	credit

Under a pooling arrangement, the current balances would be swept up into a single account, for example Account 1, and any debit balances would be cleared. In this example, this would leave Accounts 2, 3, 4 and 5 with a zero balance and Account 1 with a balance of $45,000.

By concentrating cash surpluses into a single account, Omega has the opportunity to use its cash more profitably. It can benefit from higher interest rates by investing a larger amount, or by investing some of the surplus in a long-term deposit or money market instrument.

Pooling minimizes or eliminates any overdraft that the company or group would otherwise have in its various accounts.

Arrangements for pooling can be automatic, a company's bank transferring surpluses on specified accounts to a central account at the end of each day. Alternatively, pooling can be administered by the company's own management, instructing the bank to make the required transfers between accounts.

Netting

Netting is another type of cash flow arrangement. It can be used in situations where individual business units within a company trade regularly with each other. Instead of making separate payments for every invoice from one business unit to another, only a net amount is paid or received by each unit. Netting reduces the number of payments or receipts to one per business unit.

Example
Alpha, Beta, Gamma and Delta are four divisions of Epsilon Group, trading regularly with each other. A netting arrangement is used where inter-divisional debts at the end of each month are settled on the fifth working day of the following month.

At the end of November, the following amounts were owed.

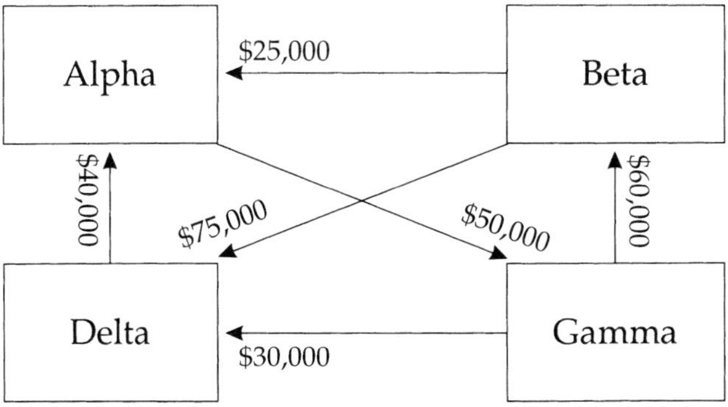

Analysis

Under a netting arrangement, there would be a single net payment from or to each division on the fifth working day of December. These payments would be organized and channeled through a netting center, perhaps a central treasury department or a bank.

	Owes	Is Owed	Net
	$	$	$
Alpha	–50,000	+65,000	+15,000
Beta	–100,000	+60,000	-40,000
Gamma	–90,000	+50,000	-40,000
Delta	–40,000	+105,000	+65,000

Payments would be as follows:

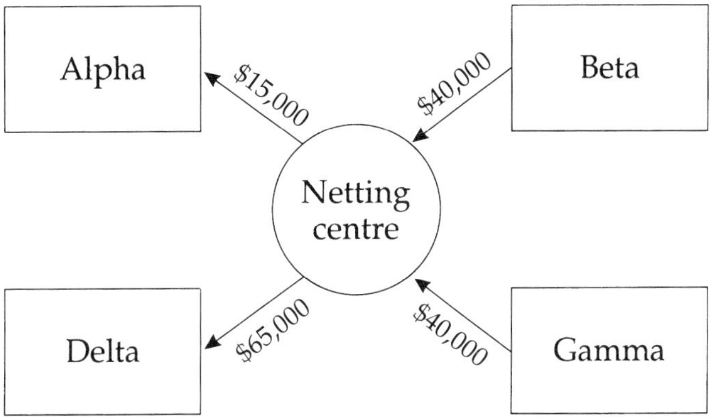

The benefits of netting include greater predictability of cash flows within the group. Netting payments occur at regular intervals. Each division must pay other divisions in full for amounts due and can expect to receive payments in full. One division, therefore, cannot ease its own cash flow problems by delaying payments to another division.

Cash Flow Control and Currency Risk Management

Companies with cash flows in several currencies have exposures to currency risk. This is the risk of losses from adverse movements in exchange rates.

Example 1

Losses can be incurred by holding cash in one currency instead of another. Suppose for example that Alpha, a UK company, has $120,000 in a US dollar account, and the exchange rate moves from $1.60 = £1 to $2 = £1.

Analysis

The sterling value of the dollars will fall from £75,000 ($120,000 ÷ 1.60) to £60,000 ($120,000 ÷ 2) because of the weakening dollar. Alpha could have avoided the £15,000 loss by switching the dollars into sterling when the exchange rate was $1.60.

Example 2

Losses can be incurred by agreeing to accept payment in one currency instead of another, or by paying for goods in one currency instead of another. Suppose that Beta buys goods from a Swiss customer and agrees to make the payment in Swiss francs. The price of the goods was SFr300,000. Assume the goods were bought on April 1 when the exchange rate was SFr2.45 = £1, and three months credit was allowed by the supplier. When payment was made on July 1, the exchange rate was SFr2.30 = £1.

Analysis

Beta bought the goods for an expected sterling price of £122,448 (SFr300,000 ÷ 2.45) but by July 1, the cost of buying the required Swiss francs had gone up to £130,434 (SFr300,000 ÷ 2.30). Beta has suffered a loss of £7,986. By agreeing to pay in Swiss francs it has had to pay more than originally expected because the Swiss franc strengthened in value against sterling during the credit period.

Currency exposures can be reduced or eliminated in various ways, such as by fixing an exchange rate with a forward exchange contract. Another method is to manage cash receipts and payments so that, so far as is possible, receipts in each currency are used to make payments in the same currency, i.e. receipts and payments in each currency are matched.

Reinvoicing Centers

Some large multinationals have established reinvoicing centers. If a subsidiary company sells goods to a customer in what is to the subsidiary a foreign currency, the subsidiary invoices the reinvoicing center in its own currency and the reinvoicing center invoices the customer in the foreign currency. Similarly, if a subsidiary buys goods in a foreign currency, the invoice can be directed from the supplier to the reinvoicing center, that will then invoice the subsidiary in its own domestic currency. The currency risk therefore is taken away from the subsidiaries and transferred to the reinvoicing center that can manage the exposures centrally.

Example
The diagram below shows how, for a small group with subsidiaries in the

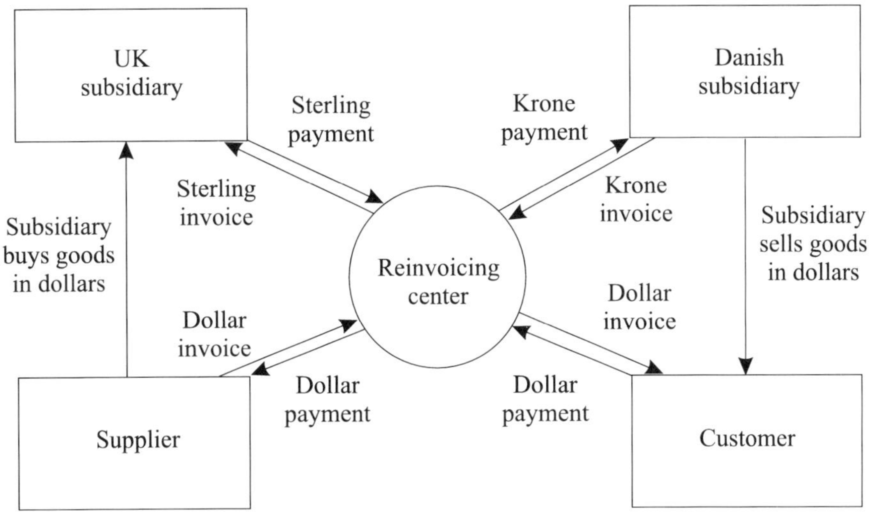

UK and Denmark, organizing currency receipts and payments through a reinvoicing center transfers the currency risk from the subsidiaries to a reinvoicing center that can be made responsible for managing the currency risk.

In this example, the UK subsidiary buys goods in dollars from a supplier. The supplier invoices the reinvoicing center in dollars, and the center invoices the subsidiary in sterling. The Danish subsidiary sells goods in dollars to a customer, but sends an invoice to the reinvoicing center in krone. The reinvoicing center sends a dollar invoice to the customer. The UK and Danish subsidiaries have no currency risk because their receipts and payments are in domestic currency. The risk, that takes the form of receiving sterling and dollars, and paying in krone and dollars, is concentrated in and managed by the reinvoicing center.

In practice, reinvoicing centers deal in many currencies and with many subsidiaries, and the example here is a simplified illustration.

Policy Issues

Although individual business units might have responsibility for day-to-day cash management, policies for cash management should be formulated centrally.

For example, a central treasury or head office should determine policy about bank accounts, borrowing arrangements and the use of surplus cash balances.

Cash management policies, of which cash flow control is an integral part, should be reviewed from time to time, particularly in large organizations, to determine whether better ways exist for handling receipts and payments, for using funds within the company or group, or for controlling cash flows. These subjects are discussed in Cash Management Audit in Chapter 8.

Consequences of Poor Cash Flow Control

If cash management is badly organized and/or controlled, the consequences could be costly, either in terms of increased costs or forsaken revenues. First, company profits will be lower. Float times and the cash collection cycle could be too long, tying up funds in working capital when there should be cash available to reduce an overdraft or to invest. For example, suppliers are paid before the end of the permitted credit period.

Idle cash balances might not be invested, or cash within the group might not be pooled, resulting in unnecessary overdraft charges. A lack of proper control can be evident in bad office procedures and practices. Cash could be misappropriated or misplaced, for example. Checks from customers can be put into a desk drawer and forgotten or, more commonly, a dishonest employee could pocket cash payments made by customers. Payments could be made without authorization or could be for incorrect amounts. Unauthorized payments could be fraudulent, but are more likely to be unnecessary and badly conceived expenditures that simply add to costs, even though the reasons for making them might be honest. Incorrect payments can happen surprisingly often; for example, paying $1,000 instead of $100, or paying the same invoice twice.

Creating a Cash Conscious Culture

Cash management within a company will benefit from a cash conscious culture that must originate with top management. Cash consciousness means an awareness that the financial health of the company depends on efficient cash flow and liquidity management. There should be a good reason for any spending. Before any expenditure is authorized, there are three basic questions that should be asked.

- Is spending on this item necessary?
- Could we get what we need by spending less – is there a cheaper alternative that is just as good?
- Does the expenditure have to be made now or can it wait?

There should be consciousness, too, about income. It is a convention of accounting that profits are earned when the sale is made. However, they are not fully secured until the cash is received from the sale. There is a risk of bad debts that vigorous collection procedures could help to reduce. Cash must come in so that a company can pay its way, and receipts should be banked as quickly as possible in order to reduce interest charges or to earn interest.

Creating a cash conscious culture can be encouraged by imposing cash limits on management spending, or by making managers accountable for cash flow control. Limits on spending can be defined in the budget. Alternatively, targets can be set for cash balances in the bank accounts of each business unit, and managers rewarded in part according to their success in achieving their target.

Internal Controls for Cash Management

The financial director of a company has a responsibility for ensuring that controls over cash are adequate and properly applied on a day-to-day basis. Control over cash management can be achieved by applying eight long-established principles of internal control. These are taught to accountancy students and learned by mnemonics such as OAP SPASM or SPAM SOAP.

The eight principles of internal control are:

O Organization and procedural controls

A Authorization

P Physical controls

S Segregation of duties

P Personnel controls

A Accounting and arithmetic controls

S Supervision

M Management controls

Organization and Procedural Controls

The organization for cash management should have a clear structure of allocated authority, responsibility, and lines of reporting. Routines and procedures should be strictly enforced. Every individual must know what he or she can and can't do, and must or must not do. For example, the person responsible for paying in checks has to be made aware that checks must be banked on the day of receipt.

Authorization

There should be a limited number of individuals authorized to sign checks and to make bank transfers. Two signatures might be required on checks over $2,000.

Physical Controls

Physical controls should be applied to restrict the access of unauthorized staff to check books and petty cash. Valuable items should be kept in a secure place until required. Physical restrictions also should exist if possible to access to cash registers, or to any room with an electronic banking system terminal. Various offices should be designated secure areas with access limited to authorized personnel only. These areas should be kept locked when empty.

Segregation of Duties

No single person should be responsible for authorizing, making, recording, and monitoring cash payments. Where applicable, the cashier responsible for handling cash payments/receipts should not be the bookkeeper who records the transactions in the cashbook, nor the person responsible for authorizing payments.

Personnel Controls

Employees who will be handling cash receipts and payments should be screened as potential security risks before their appointment. References from previous employers should be checked.

Accounting and Arithmetic Controls

There should be rules and procedures for making detailed checks on the accuracy and completeness of transactions; for example checks that settlement discounts have been properly calculated, and routine checks that all payments have been properly authorized.

Supervision

Ideally there should be regular supervision by responsible officials of day-to-day cash transactions.

Management Controls

Managers should be responsible for the proper functioning of all cash management controls through a system of regular reporting, analysis and review. This should include budgeting and budgetary control reports, *ad hoc* checks, etc.

Good management is a key requirement for effective security and controls because management must be responsible for making sure that controls are adequate, that they are exercised and that they work as well as can be expected.

"No internal control system, however elaborate, can by itself guarantee efficient administration and the completeness and accuracy of the records, nor can it be proof against fraudulent collusion, especially on the part of those holding positions of authority or trust. 1. Internal controls depending on segregation of duties can be avoided by collusion. 2. Authorization controls can be abused by the person in whom the authority is vested. 3. While the competence and integrity of the personnel operating the controls may be ensured by selection and training, these qualities may alter due to pressure exerted both within and without the enterprise. 4. Human error due to errors of judgment or interpretation, to misunderstanding, carelessness, fatigue, or distraction may undermine the effective operation of internal controls."

Auditing Guideline, Internal Controls

Authorization Controls

It is critical in this era of electronic funds transfer and computer fraud that tight control be exercised over the authorization of payments and the establishment of new bank accounts. Authorization controls are vital to cash management, and within a medium-to-large organization, there should be a documented authorizations system.

The responsibility for authorizing expenditures must be explicit. No one should be able to make spending decisions for which he or she is not properly authorized. Authorization powers are normally delegated, but there should be a limit on the amount of expenditure that an individual can authorize without referring the item to a superior for approval. Limits on authorization should go up the management hierarchy to the board of directors. A distinction could be made between capital expenditures and revenue expenditures, with different authorization limits for each.

All authorized expenditures should be documented. If a subordinate asks a superior to approve an expenditure because it exceeds his own authorization limit, he should be required to submit a documented request for spending authorization that should be signed by the superior as evidence of approval. Invoices from suppliers should be checked and initialed by the individual authorizing the expenditure, to confirm that the invoice is accurate and should be paid.

There should be an authorization system for payments procedures. Individuals who are authorized to sign checks should be mandated senior managers, directors perhaps, in the company. One individual might be permitted to sign checks up to a specified limit. Checks above a certain limit could require the signature of two authorized individuals, or the chairman or chief executive of the company. No check should be signed without confirming first that the expenditure itself has been authorized.

A limited number of individuals – perhaps just two – should have the authority (voice powers) to instruct the company's bank by telephone to transfer funds. Their voice must be recognizable to the official at the bank with whom they deal. Authorizations by telephone subsequently should be confirmed in writing, preferably with two signatures.

There must be strict controls over the authorization of new bank accounts. At least two signatures from a restricted number of authorized individuals should be required to open or close an account. In many major companies, all new bank accounts and major banking transactions have to receive the prior sanction of a sub-committee of the board of directors.

Banks will require *mandates* for each account, specifying

- the number of signatures required for each check, for example one signature for checks up to $1,000 in value, and two signatures for checks of higher value
- samples of each signature
- how telephone instructions to make transfers are initiated, by whom, and how many signatures should be required on the subsequent written confirmation
- the individual or department to which confirmation of transactions should be sent, preferably not an authorized signatory.

Electronic Banking

Establishing and managing payment authorization controls are prime elements of security in electronic banking systems.

Security can be provided and managed by defining a range or hierarchy of passwords that can be updated at regular intervals or constantly updated on a real-time basis. Only authorized personnel will be given the senior passwords permitting them to access specific function menus needed to initiate a funds transfer. Unlike telephone-initiated transfers, electronic funds transfers do not require written confirmation. This means that a password management and updating system needs to be implemented, and that the authorized individual gets the payment details correct, including the account number to be credited, without the benefit of a check from a second person.

Summary

Cash flow control is an integral part of the broader cash management responsibility. A distinction can be made between responsibilities for operational cash flows and for financing and investing cash flows.

The responsibilities for receipts, payments and cash balances could be shared between local business units and head office, perhaps a central treasury department in a multinational group, that might be an offshore company. Head office should define cash management policy. For companies or groups with multiple bank accounts, perhaps in different countries and currencies, a centralized organization of banking arrangements often will be desirable. A central treasury could administer arrangements for pooling, netting and a reinvoicing center, and also be responsible for currency risk management.

Whatever organization is adopted for cash management, suitable controls should be applied.

The Cash Flow Cycle

It has to be a general rule of business that the cash received from selling goods and services should exceed the cash paid out to make and provide them. Cash payments are made in the expectation of eventually receiving a larger amount of cash in the future. Some of these cash receipts can then be spent to make more goods or provide more services for sale. Thus, there is a continuing business cycle of buying and selling, and paying for purchases and being paid for sales. This rudimentary analysis of business explains the concept of the cash cycle.

Cash Cycle

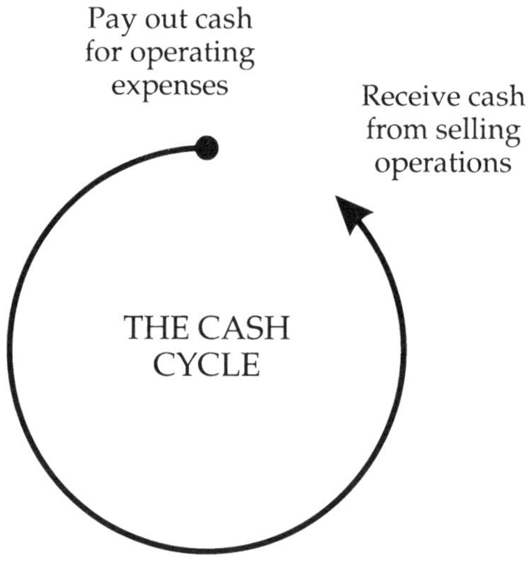

Management is responsible for ensuring that:

- cash income exceeds cash expenditures (profit management)
- cash income is received as quickly as possible and the duration of the cash cycle is as short or as quick as possible (cash management)
- cash is available to meet due payments and is put to good use when it is received from sales (cash management).

The cash cycle is linked to the trading cycle. In a manufacturing company, the trading cycle begins with the purchase of raw materials, goes through production and the warehousing of finished goods prior to sale, and ends with the eventual sale of the manufactured goods. The cash cycle, in contrast, starts with the payment for raw materials and ends with the receipt of payments from customers.

In a retailing company, the trading cycle starts with the purchase of stock for resale and ends with the sale of the stock. The cash cycle runs from payment for the stock to the receipt of cash from customer sales, although some retailers can sell stock before they have to pay for it.

In most businesses, purchases from external suppliers start the trading cycle and payments to suppliers start the cash cycle. However, there are many payments that don't go to suppliers of materials and components. Wages and salaries are paid to employees. Overhead expenses include payments for rent, rates, telephones, advertising and consultancy fees. Even for these items there is a cash cycle because of the time gap between making payments and obtaining cash income from the sales that the expenditures support.

Cash Flow Time Line

The trading cycle and the cash flow cycle are measured by time. The trading cycle is the time from purchasing raw materials until the finished goods are sold, and the cash flow cycle is the time from the first cash expenditures to the eventual receipt of payments from sales. These cycles can be superimposed on each other and illustrated on a line that represents the passage of time – a time line.

Different types of business have their own trading cycle and cash-cycle characteristics. A manufacturing company offers the simplest way to illustrate a time line.

Cash Flow Time Line: Manufacturing Business

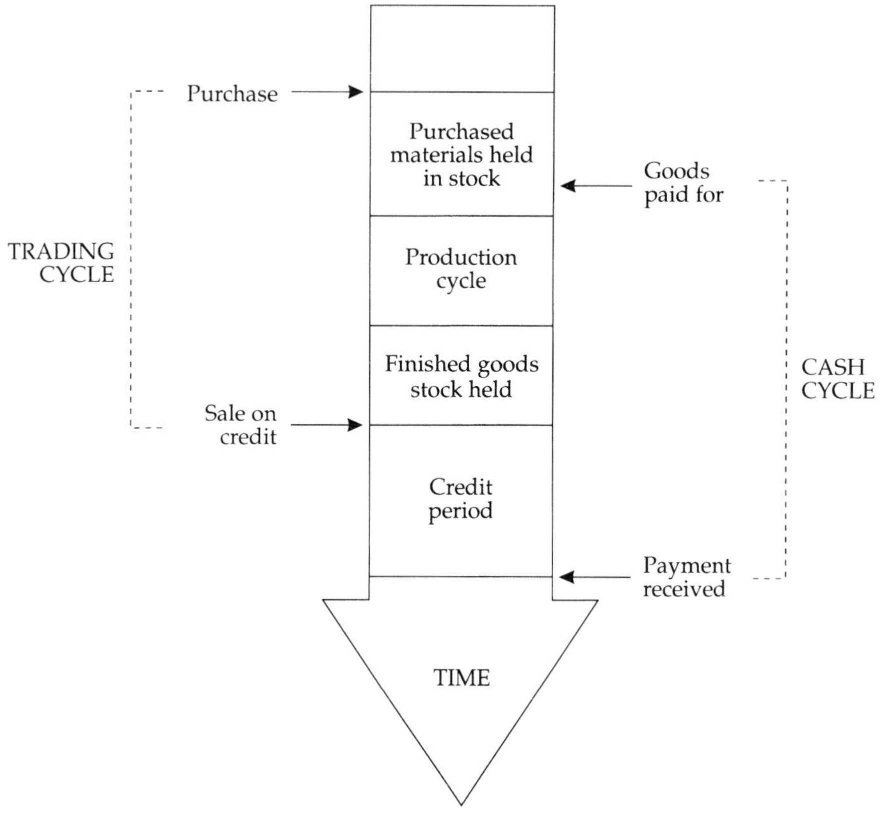

The cash cycle or time line varies in length according to the duration of each item on the line.

There are three main elements in the cash cycle and time line

- holding stocks, from their purchase from external suppliers, through the production and warehousing of finished goods, up to the time of sale

- taking time to pay suppliers and other creditors
- allowing customers (debtors) time to pay.

In a retailing business, most sales are for cash, by credit card or debit card, and the company therefore receives most of its cash income at the time of sale. Large supermarket chains that sell goods within a few days of purchase might not pay their suppliers until after the goods have been sold and the cash received.

Cash Flow Time Line: Supermarket Chain

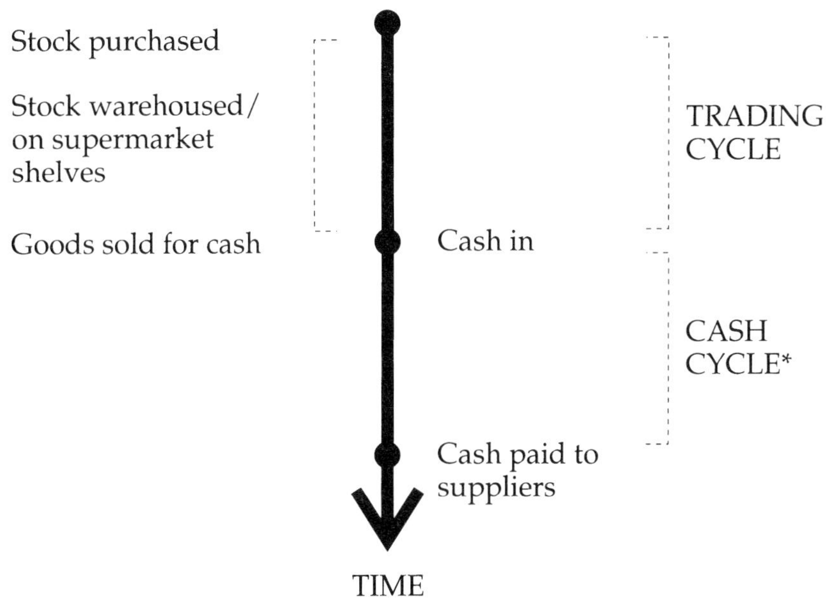

* Negative, because cash income is received before expenditures are paid for

Working Capital

Working capital, or circulating capital, is the amount of funds required to support the day-to-day operations of a business. A simple definition of working capital normally used in relation to the cash cycle is the value of stocks plus debtors and minus creditors.

	Stocks
+	Debtors
–	Creditors
=	Working Capital

Changes in the length of the cash cycle have a direct effect on the amount of working capital required. A longer cash cycle would result from holding stock for an extended period before it is used or sold, a longer production cycle, customers taking longer to pay or paying suppliers more quickly. If stock is held longer before use or sale, there will be an increase in inventory. Similarly, if the production cycle slows down, there will be more costs, including materials and labor, etc., tied up in work-in-progress. The volume of debtors will increase if customers take longer to pay, and there will be fewer creditors if suppliers are paid more quickly.

Example

Alpha sells $100,000 of goods on credit every month. Customers used to pay on average after one month, but economic difficulties have increased the average time to pay to two months.

Analysis

The average cash flow cycle has slowed down by one month because customers are taking longer to pay. At any time, Alpha can now expect to have $200,000 of unpaid debts instead of $100,000 as before.

The consequent cash cycle changes are summarized in the table.

Consequences of Changes in the Cash Cycle

Longer cash cycle	Shorter cash cycle
Stocks held longer before use or sale – more stocks are held	Stocks held a shorter time – fewer stocks are held
Production cycle longer – work-in-progress will increase	Production cycle shorter – less work-in-progress
Debtors take longer to pay – there will be more debtors	Debtors pay more quickly – there will be fewer debtors
Shorter time to pay creditors – there will be fewer creditors	Longer period of credit taken from/ allowed by creditors – there will be more creditors

Changes in the cash cycle also affect a company's cash flows. A lengthening of the cash cycle, with more stocks and debtors or fewer creditors, will slow down cash receipts. A shorter cash cycle, with fewer stocks and debtors or more creditors, will speed up a company's cash receipts and should improve its cash balances.

Working Capital Changes and Cash Balances

Longer cash cycle	Shorter cash cycle
More working capital (stocks + debtors - creditors)	Less working capital (stocks + debtors - creditors)
Worse cash balance	Improved cash balance

This point can be illustrated with a simple example.

Example

Beta, a merchant, received an order from a customer for a quantity of goods. The goods were to be sold to the customer in two equal deliveries, the first in June and the second in August. Beta purchased all the goods that the customer ordered in a single consignment, at the beginning of June, and paid the supplier $10,000 immediately.

The first delivery of goods to the customer took place on schedule in June, and the customer was invoiced $7,000, with credit terms of 30 days' net.

Analysis

When the first delivery of goods to the customer took place, Beta earned a profit of $2,000 ($7,000 minus cost of $5,000). Beta's cash position, however, was $10,000 worse off than before the consignment was purchased, because the supplier had been paid but half the goods were still unsold and in stock, and the customer had not yet paid for the other half.

The increase in working capital has created a reduction in cash balances.

	$
Stock increase (unsold stock)	+5,000
Debtors increase	+7,000
	+12,000
Creditors (no change)	–
Increase in working capital	+12,000
Reduction in cash balance	–10,000

The difference between the lower cash balance of $10,000 and the increase in working capital of $12,000 can be explained by the profit element of $2,000 in the valuation of Beta's debtor. If the debtor had been valued at the cost of sale ($5,000 rather than at sale value), the increase in working capital would have been $10,000, directly explaining the reduction in the cash balance.

Measuring Cash Cycle Time

A company ought to monitor the length of its cash cycle. There are two ways of measuring cash cycle time:

- sampling
- ratio measurements.

Sampling

Sampling is a more laborious method of measurement, but is likely to produce better information about payment times for debtors and creditors. By sampling debtors, a profile can be built up of the typical time from issuing an invoice to payment by the customer. An average time to pay can be established from the sample, for all customers taken together, and also for different groups of customers such as domestic corporate customers, domestic non-corporate customers and export customers.

Similarly, a sample of supplier payments can be taken to establish the average time from receipt of invoice to making the payment. The sample can be sub-divided into groups of suppliers with common characteristics; for example, suppliers who ask for payment within 15 days of invoice, those who allow 30 days, etc. Credit terms offered by the supplier and the credit period taken are not necessarily the same. Employees are a form of creditor, and the average time to pay will depend on the mix of weekly paid and monthly paid staff.

Ratio Measurements

Ratio measurements are a quicker method of analyzing cash cycle times. The ratios are derived from an analysis of the company's accounts. The measurements are only approximations, but could be sufficiently accurate. An advantage of ratio measurements over sampling cash cycle times is that an estimate can be obtained for stock turnover time as well as debtor and creditor payment periods.

The measurements that can be obtained by ratio analysis from data in a company's balance sheet and profit and loss account are

- stock turnover period
- debtor days, average time taken to pay by customers
- average time taken to pay creditors.

For a manufacturing company, the stock turnover period can be sub-divided into a turnover period for raw material stock, a production cycle time, and a turnover period for finished goods stock.

Ratio measurements are derived from the accounts of a company for a given time period, typically one year. Assuming a 365-day year and annual figures for sales and the cost of sales, the following ratio measurements can be obtained:

Stock turnover period $$\frac{\text{Average stock}}{\text{Cost of goods sold in the year}} \times 365 \text{ days}$$

Debtor days (debtors' payment period) $$\frac{\text{Average trade debtors}}{\text{Sales in the year}} \times 365 \text{ days}$$

Credit period from creditors $$\frac{\text{Average trade creditors}}{\text{Sales in the year}} \times 365 \text{ days}$$

Ratios can seem complex or puzzling when presented as a formula, but the underlying logic is quite simple. Suppose, for example, that a retail company turns over stock costing \$365 million every year, an average of \$1 million each day, assuming a 365-day year. If the company has stock in hand costing \$6 million, it is holding six days' worth of stock. This is the stock turnover period. The ratio would be calculated as \$6 million ÷ \$365 million x 365 days = 6 days.

The same simple concept applies to average debtor days and the average credit period taken from trade creditors.

Average figures for stocks, debtors and creditors can be estimated as the average of the beginning-of-the-year and end-of-the-year amounts, both obtainable from the company's balance sheet. There will, of course, be seasonal peaks and troughs throughout the year depending on the type or seasonality of the business.

The stock turnover period for a manufacturing company can be sub-divided into three ratios:

Raw material stock turnover period $$\frac{\text{Average raw material stock}}{\text{Cost of goods sold in the year}} \times 365 \text{ days}$$

\+ Production cycle $$\frac{\text{Average work-in-progress}}{\text{Cost of goods sold in the year}} \times 365 \text{ days}$$

+ Finished goods stock turnover period $\dfrac{\text{Average finished goods stock}}{\text{Cost of goods sold in the year}} \times 365$ days

The cost-of-goods-sold figure is used to calculate the ratios both for stock turnover and the average period of credit from suppliers. This is because cost of goods sold is readily obtainable from a company's published accounts. More accurate measurements, if the data were available from the company's detailed management accounts, would be:

Raw material stock turnover $\dfrac{\text{Average raw material stock}}{\text{Cost of material purchases in the period}} \times 365$ days

Production cycle $\dfrac{\text{Average work-in-progress}}{\text{Cost of production in the period}} \times 365$ days

Credit period from creditors $\dfrac{\text{Average trade creditors}}{\text{Cost of purchases on credit in the period}} \times 365$ days

Ratio measurements are approximations of averages, and can provide only an estimate of the typical cash cycle. However, if the same method of measurement is used consistently, the information should be reliable for comparing changes and trends from one year to the next. Management should be able to infer, for example, whether the cash cycle is getting longer or shorter.

The turnover times obtained, by sampling or ratio measurements, can be combined to produce an estimate of the overall cash cycle time in days.

Raw material stock turnover
+ Production cycle
+ Finished goods turnover
= Stock turnover
+ Debtor days
– Average time to pay suppliers
= Cash Cycle

Example

The following data has been taken from the published accounts of Gamma Group, a major manufacturing group.

	Current year	Previous year	Average
	$m	$m	$m
Raw materials	53.1	44.9	49.0
Work in progress	36.2	28.0	32.1
Finished goods	83.6	83.7	83.65
Trade debtors	220.4	183.8	202.1
Trade creditors	74.9	68.0	71.45
Sales	979.4		
Cost of sales	681.7		

Using ratio measurements, what is the cash cycle time of the company?

Analysis

The estimated length of the cash cycle time is as follows:

		Days
Raw material stock turnover	49 ÷ 681.7 × 365	26
Production cycle	32.1 ÷ 681.7 × 365	17
Finished goods stock turnover	83.65 ÷ 681.7 × 365	45
Total stock turnover time		88
Debt collection time (average)	202.1 ÷ 979.4 × 365	75
		163
Credit taken from suppliers (average)	71.45 ÷ 681.7 × 365	(38)
Cash cycle		125

The cash cycle can be monitored over time. If annual accounts are used to measure the ratios, the cash cycle can be monitored once a year. Unless there are substantial changes in business operations, the length of the cycle ought to remain fairly stable. Any changes that do occur ought to be thoroughly investigated.

Benefits of a Shorter Cash Cycle

The possible benefits of reducing the cash cycle time can be illustrated using the same example. Let's suppose that Gamma's management decide the 125-day cash cycle is too long and that the following average periods could be achieved and sustained:

Raw material stock turnover	24 days
Production cycle	16 days
Finished goods stock turnover	40 days
Debt collection period	60 days
Credit from suppliers	42 days

If turnover and cost of sales are unchanged, it is possible to estimate the amount of stocks, debtors and creditors that the business would have.

		Achievable	Current	Difference
		$m	$m	$m
Raw materials	(24 ÷ 365 × 681.7)	44.8	53.1	–8.3
Work in progress	(16 ÷ 365 × 681.7)	29.9	36.2	–6.3
Finished goods	(40 ÷ 365 × 681.7)	74.7	83.6	–8.9
Stock total		149.4	172.9	–23.5
Debtors	(60 ÷ 365 × 979.4)	161.0	220.4	–59.4
		310.4	393.3	–82.9
Creditors	(42 ÷ 365 × 681.7)	(78.4)	(74.9)	–3.5
		232.0	318.4	–86.4

In this situation, the company would be able to reduce its working capital by about $86 million by shortening the length of the cash cycle as planned. Cash to the value of $86.4 million would flow into the company more quickly than if the cycle time had not changed, and the company's cash balances would increase by this amount.

In practice, a company should be able to use management accounts to obtain better data, and to carry out a separate cash cycle analysis for each major product line more frequently than once each year.

Is there an Optimum Cash Cycle Length?

Measuring a cash cycle alone doesn't provide answers to any key management questions, but management should want to know

- whether the cash cycle is too long, and investment in working capital should be reduced by shortening the cycle, or
- whether the cash cycle is too short and becoming unsustainable, indicating a need at some time in the future for an increase in working capital investment.

The answers to these questions will vary according to each company's situation. A combination of three approaches can be adopted to monitor and control the cash cycle. Management could

- monitor changes in the cash cycle over time, substantial changes would indicate that something significant has happened
- measure and monitor the company's liquidity position and liquidity risk;
- look in detail at stock turnover, payments procedures and collection procedures, with a view to improving times.

These approaches to cash-cycle management are described in more detail in the next chapter.

Managing Liquidity and the Cash Flow Cycle

The size of a company's investment in working capital depends on a number of factors.

These include

- volume of sales. Higher business volume means more stocks, debtors and creditors, thus more working capital required
- inflation. Inflation increases the value of stocks and debtors, thus more money is tied up in working capital
- length of the cash cycle.

For our purposes, the issue to consider is whether management action can reduce working capital requirements, and improve cash balances, by reducing the length of the cash cycle. Efficient management of working capital can result in improved liquidity by deferring payments, speeding up payments from debtors, and reducing stock turnover times.

A shorter cash-cycle time will reduce the amount of cash that a company needs to invest in its business. For example, suppose a company has an average cash cycle of three months, and needs to invest $30 million in stocks and debtors to support operational activity for the three months between paying for expenditures and receiving payments from customers. If it were able to reduce the cash cycle to an average of two months, its investment to support operating activities would fall to $20 million ($120 million x 2/12), thus releasing funds of $10 million. An interest rate benefit would arise from lower borrowings by the company, or higher income from investing the released cash.

A company should aim to make the cash cycle as short as possible, but only if the length of the cash cycle achieved can be sustained in the foreseeable future without damaging operational efficiency. If a cash cycle is shortened by running down stocks or building up debts to suppliers, in a way that cannot be sustained or is operationally harmful, the cycle will have to lengthen again eventually, and all cash flow benefits will be lost. Worse still, if the company doesn't have the cash or borrowing facilities available when the cash cycle lengthens again, it will face a liquidity crisis and possibly be forced out of business.

Liquidity

Liquidity is the amount of cash a company has in hand, or can lay its hands on quickly to meet its obligations. It consists of cash and items that can be cashed quickly, such as money-market investments, time deposits, and unused bank overdraft facilities.

Arguably, debtors are liquid assets because they should pay what they owe in the near future. In addition, stocks are often fairly liquid assets because they should soon be sold. However, stocks are not as liquid as debtors, except in fast turnover businesses, such as consumer goods retailing.

A company needs enough cash coming in to meet payments when they fall due. As a general rule, it should be possible to sustain sufficient liquidity from day-to-day operations provided that these are profitable, although there can be occasional large calls on cash resources, perhaps to purchase new fixed assets.

If a company doesn't have the cash to make due payments, it should have borrowing facilities in place and be reasonably confident that the bank won't insist that it reduce its overdraft before it is in a position to do so.

A lack of liquidity can be a serious financial risk. The need to sustain liquidity to meet payment obligations can act as a constraint on measures to reduce the cash cycle time.

Measuring Liquidity

The liquidity position of a company can be monitored by preparing cash forecasts. Measures could be taken to fund a forecast cash deficit by borrowing, or to reduce a cash deficit by postponing or canceling a capital expenditure project, or by cutting discretionary spending such as expenditure on advertising and public relations.

Current liabilities must be paid in the near future, and a company should expect the cash in order to make the payments to come from its operating receipts. The company's capacity to generate cash can be judged from its current assets, relative to the size of its current liabilities. A company's liquidity therefore can be monitored by financial ratio measurements. The purpose of liquidity ratio measurements is to alert management to improving or deteriorating liquidity. Changes in liquidity might not be fully apparent from cash flow forecasts.

The most common ratios used to monitor liquidity are the current ratio and the quick ratio, also called the acid-test ratio.

The current ratio is the ratio of a company's current assets, including cash and short-term investments, to its current liabilities.

$$\text{Current ratio} = \frac{\text{Current assets}}{\text{Current liabilities*}}$$

**Current liabilities are the amount in the company's balance sheet for creditors' amounts falling due within one year.*

The quick ratio is similar to the current ratio, except that stocks are excluded from current assets because they are less liquid, that is further back in the cash flow time line than other current assets. Moreover, stocks can vary in their ability to be readily converted into liquid cash, for example stocks of a generic nature such as oil, coal, or grain are more easily converted into cash than last year's best selling toy.

$$\text{Quick ratio or acid-test ratio} = \frac{\text{Current assets excluding stocks}}{\text{Current liabilities}}$$

An increase in either of these ratios over time indicates increasing liquidity. Falling ratios indicate diminishing liquidity.

An Ideal Liquidity Ratio?

Accountancy students traditionally have been taught that there is an ideal minimum current ratio of 2.0 and an ideal minimum acid-test ratio of 1.0, and if a company's ratios fall below these amounts, it is likely to have a serious liquidity problem.

There is some truth in this generalization because a low liquidity ratio and a low acid-test ratio are often caused by a large bank overdraft or by high short-term borrowings. Even so, these ideal minimum levels are often inappropriate to a company's particular situation and some companies with much lower ratios can operate indefinitely without cash flow difficulties. It is more important to establish whether the ratios are stable and sustainable, or whether they are deteriorating progressively. A liquidity ratio that remains at about 0.6 from one year to the next could indicate greater stability than a current ratio that has fallen to 2.1 from 3.5 the previous year.

In some cases, an average ratio is used. This variant simply calculates the average between the same ratio taken at two different points in time. Here, the idea is to try to smooth out seasonal or yearly variations to get a more realistic view of the typical level of the ratio. Seasonal variations, for example, can affect industries such as agriculture, toys and tourism. Similarly, annual variations can affect industries with long asset conversion cycles (raw material to finished goods) such as shipbuilding, aerospace, and construction.

Example
Alpha's reported balance sheet shows the following information:

	Current Year	Previous Year
	$000	$000
Current assets		
Stocks	3,398	1,946
Debtors	13,592	11,987
Cash at bank and in hand	8,346	3,752
	25,336	17,685
Creditors: amounts falling due within one year	20,566	17,603
Net current assets	4,770	82

Analysis
The company's liquidity ratios are as follows:

	Current Year	Previous Year
Current ratio	$\frac{25,336}{20,566} = 1.23$	$\frac{17,685}{17,603} = 1.00$
Quick ratio	$\frac{(25,336 - 3,398)}{20,566} = 1.07$	$\frac{(17,685 - 1,946)}{17,603} = 0.89$

Alpha's current ratio is fairly low, but has improved since the previous year. The quick ratio also has improved, and it could be inferred therefore that the company's liquidity is good. The improvement in the liquidity ratios is the result of the large increase in cash, from $3.752 million to $8.346 million, and it is not clear from the information available where the cash has come from.

Liquidity and the Cash Flow Cycle

In its trading operations, a company creates liquidity through the cash cycle, paying for raw materials, labor and other resources, converting them into goods or services for sale and obtaining payment from customers. A profitable company with a regular flow of trade should be able to remain liquid, and accumulate cash surpluses from its profits.

A regular cash cycle should enable a company to sustain its liquidity, regardless of its liquidity ratios. However, stability in the ratios over time would be an indication that the cash cycle is regular.

Loss of liquidity could arise from an inability to sell goods, or even an inability to collect payments from debtors. If a company is unable to sell goods and services, its stock turnover period is likely to lengthen, as unsold stocks build up. The quick ratio is likely to fall, as the number of debtors declines and the list of unpaid creditors gets longer.

Therefore a change in the cash flow cycle time is more likely to result in a change in liquidity.

Example
Beta has an annual sales turnover of $50 million. Its most recent annual operating profit was $5 million, as follows:

	$ million
Turnover	50
Cost of sales	–30
	20
Distribution and administration expenses	–15
Operating profit	5

Current assets and current liabilities are as follows:

Stocks	3
Debtors	4
Cash at bank and in hand	1
Short-term creditors	8
Net current assets	4
	12

There is no bank overdraft.

Analysis

Taking the company's current position, liquidity seems satisfactory. The current ratio is 2:1 and the quick ratio is 5:4 (1.25:1). It can be calculated that the average stock turnover period is 1.2 months ($\frac{3}{30}$ × 12) and the average time for debtors to pay is 0.96 months ($\frac{4}{50}$ × 12). Suppose however that the company's stock turnover and debtors' payment times were both longer, and that stock turnover averaged three months and average debtor days were two months. The current assets and current liabilities would be as follows:

	Total	Change
	$ million	$ million
Stocks ($\frac{3}{12}$ × £30 million)	7.5	+4.5
Debtors ($\frac{2}{12}$ × £50 million)	8.3	+4.3
Cash	0	–1.0
	15.8	+7.8
Short-term creditors (no change)	(4.0)	–
Bank overdraft	(7.8)	(7.8)
Net current assets	4.0	–

The increase in stocks and debtors by $8.8 million ($4.5m + $4.3m) has to be funded. Unless there is funding from another source, for example cash from continuing profits on trade, a bank loan, a share issue or the sale of fixed assets, the money would have to come from lower cash balances or a bank overdraft. In this example, the increase in stocks and debtors of $8.8 million has been funded by the original cash of $1 million and a bank overdraft of $7.8 million. The company's liquidity is therefore much worse, with a current ratio of 1.34 (15.8:11.8) and a quick ratio of 0.70 (8.3:11.8).

Suppose, however, that the company now obtained a long-term bank loan of $7.8 million to pay off the overdraft. Its liquidity position would be restored and the balance sheet would be as follows:

	$ million
Stocks	7.5
Debtors	8.3
	15.8
Short-term creditors	–4.0
	11.8

The current ratio now would be 3.95 (15.8:4) and the quick ratio 2.08 (8.3:4). The increase in these ratios could indicate excessive liquidity and a cash cycle that is too long.

This example has been oversimplified because the changes in the cash cycle have been applied to a static balance sheet. In reality, the company's cash position would be continually affected by other factors, such as profits from trading and capital expenditures. The purpose of the example is to show that there is a connection between liquidity and the cash cycle, and that unless a company has sufficient cash in hand or ready access to other funding sources, a longer cash cycle could reduce liquidity by forcing it to borrow on overdraft. On the other hand, if extra working capital is financed by long-term funding such as a bank loan, a high liquidity ratio could indicate excessive working capital and a cash cycle that is too long. A cause for concern should be a high current ratio or acid-test ratio that has risen substantially from an already high level.

The Overtrading Company

When a company is expanding rapidly, it might operate at a profit but still suffer from a cash flow problem because of the requirement for more working capital to finance the expanding business. It could then be trading at a higher volume than it can safely support with its financial resources, and would be overtrading.

Example
A trading company achieves the following annual results:

	$ million
Sales	140
Costs of sales	120
Trading profit	20

Average stocks are one sixth of the annual costs of sales, and stock turnover is two months. Average trade creditors are one twelfth of the annual cost of sales, creditors are paid after one month. Average debtors are one quarter of annual sales and take three months to pay.

Analysis

If the company maintained annual sales and costs at this level, its operational cash flows would bring in $20 million every year, the amount of cash profit.

If the company doubled its sales in the subsequent year and cash cycle periods remained the same, the company would have negative operational cash flows of $5 million. This is because the increase in working capital would require a bigger investment than the company could fund out of its profits.

	Cash flow
	$m
Trading profit (20 × 2)	+40
(Increase) in stocks (2/12 × 120)	–20
(Increase) in debtors (3/12 × 140)	–35
Increase in trade creditors (1/12 × 120)	+10
Operational cash flow	–5

If the company does not have the financial resources to find this cash requirement for $5 million, it could be overtrading, and in danger of going into receivership.

5

Reducing Cash Cycle Time

Any measures taken to reduce the cash cycle time can provide enormous cash flow benefits, but only if the reductions are sustainable. For every $1 million of turnover, with interest rates at 10%, a reduction of just one week in the cash cycle will bring an improvement in annual profits of about $1,900 ($1m ÷ 52 × 10%). A company with annual turnover of $100 million could save around $190,000 annually by cutting the cash cycle by one week.

A cash-management approach to stocks, debtors and creditors should

- encourage better stock management
- rationalize and improve billing and collection procedures in order to minimize the time to get cash from customers into the business
- rationalize and improve payment procedures, to maximize, within reason, the time it takes to pay cash out of the business.

Stock Turnover Times

Operational managers and the purchasing department normally are responsible for stock levels. The ability of a financial controller or treasurer to help improve stock turnover times depends on the relationship built up with the line managers concerned. His or her role should be to report stock turnover times and changes in stock turnover, and to indicate how much stockholding is costing the company. Operational managers might not be aware, for example, of what the benefit would be of a 10%, or even 50%, reduction in inventory.

Stock turnover information could be presented in regular reports. Separate reports could be produced for raw materials and consumables, work in progress and finished goods. Within each report, stock items could be grouped into major categories, with minor value items ignored, depending on the way they are bought, used or sold.

Example

Finished Goods Stock Turnover – Product Line Alpha

	Current year	Previous year	Year minus 2
Average stock ($000)	600	550	580
Cost of sales ($000	2,576	2,509	2,680
Turnover period (days)	85	80	79
Change over period	+5	+1	
Interest rate	10%	12%	
Cost per day's change in turnover	$706	$825	
Effect on *profit* of change in the year (compared with previous year)	–$3,530	–$825	

Finished Goods Stock Turnover – Product Line Beta

	Current year	Previous year	Year minus 2
Average stock ($000)	1,000	800	750
Cost of sales ($000	5,984	5,309	4,845
Turnover period (days)	61	55	56.5
Change over period	+6	1.5	
Interest rate	10%	12%	
Cost per day's change in turnover	$1,639	$1,744	
Effect on *profit* of change in the year (compared with previous year)	–$9,834	+$2,614	

It may help to see how the figures in this example are derived. Amounts are shown for average stock and the cost of sales for each product line, for the current year and the previous two years. For each year, a stock turnover period is reported. The current year's average stock turnover for product line Beta, for example, is 61 days, calculated as 1,000 ÷ 5,984 × 365 days.

The reduction or increase in the average stock turnover time since the previous year is shown. The cost of the change in turnover time is reported as an interest cost, at the interest rate applicable for that year. The interest cost, or value, of an increase, or reduction, in stock turnover time arises from the resulting increase, or decrease, in stocks and the consequent change in working capital funding.

For product line Beta in the current year, the cost or value for a change of one day in the stock turnover period is $1,639 (1/365 × $5,984,000 x 10%). Because stock turnover time for Beta has increased by six days since the previous year, the company has suffered additional costs of $9,834 ($1,639 × 6).

Such reports can help line management to identify

- stock lines whose turnover period is improving or worsening
- the cost or benefit from any such change
- whether action might be justified to rectify a worsening turnover time, or consolidate improvements that have been achieved.

Just in Time

Just in time (JIT) is a technique used in manufacturing for organizing work flows to achieve rapid and flexible production to a high-quality standard while minimizing waste and stock levels. Perhaps the most well-known feature of JIT is that it is a system for reducing inventory levels and work in progress.

- Just in time production is driven by demand, and items are manufactured only when they are needed.
- Just in time purchasing is the matching of purchases as closely as possible with usage, so that stocks of raw materials and components are reduced to almost zero.

Items should be delivered or produced just in time for when they are needed. Materials or goods sitting around a factory are not making any money; they tie up capital and take up space. One of the first results of adopting JIT production should be a steep fall in inventories, and a consequent savings in interest costs from a shortening of the cash cycle.

Stocks of work in progress can be reduced through higher production quality and workflow organization. This in turn eliminates the need for inspection of goods, the reworking of defective items, shopfloor queues and unnecessary movements of materials.

Although JIT has implications for the cash flow cycle, its implementation is an operational management responsibility, with important non-financial implications such as closer supplier relationships and high-quality standards.

The production process may need to be shortened and simplified. The manufacture of components and sub-assemblies has to be synchronized so that these are available when needed, and are neither too early, causing excess stocks, nor too late, causing a production delay.

Quality could be improved through measures such as checks on output quality and the training of workers. Workers need to be trained in diverse skills so they can move from one task to another, keeping production flowing smoothly and contributing to the flexibility of work scheduling.

Just-in-time manufacturing also provides financial benefits through a short stock turnover period and low stock levels. By reporting these potential financial benefits, a cash manager might encourage operational management to move towards JIT.

It should be noted that JIT is a Japanese inventory technique. The practice originated in Japan, a relatively strike-free consensus society. US companies, in striving to maximize operational efficiency, have adopted the technique, as have some industries in Europe.

Cash Collection Cycle Time

Every department with responsibility for cash collection should have procedures for the regular review of the collection cycle. This begins with taking orders from customers, and ends with receiving the payment. It includes the dispatch of goods, or provision of services, invoicing and debtor control.

The cash collection cycle consists of eight elements, although not all of these are features of cash collection

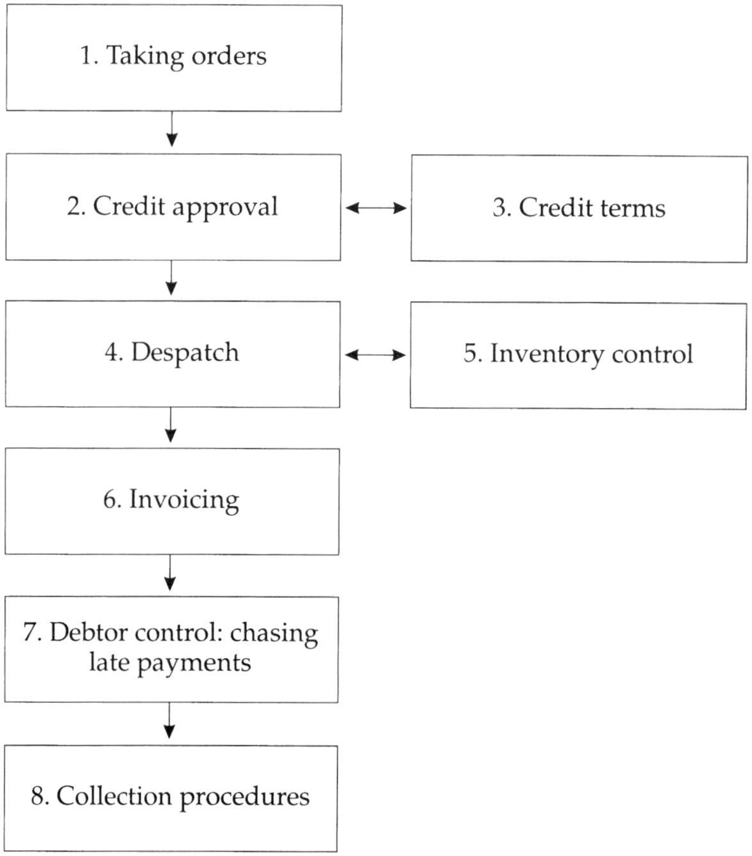

Each of these elements can be monitored, to assess whether measures are possible to improve the collection cycle time.

Taking Orders

Time can be lost in the process of taking orders. It is often worthwhile to look at the average time between obtaining an order and, after approving credit for the customer, dispatching the goods or providing the service.

Orders can be taken by a variety of methods, through direct selling, by letter, by telephone, with or without written confirmation, the internet, electronically, or over the counter. Some methods for taking orders are much quicker than others, and customers could be encouraged to use these methods especially because it is usually in the customer's interest to have an order processed quickly. Orders by fax can be encouraged, for example, by giving a fax number prominence in sales literature. A company that insists on written confirmation of a telephone order might consider whether it is necessary to delay dispatch until after the confirmation has been received.

Sales representatives should try to secure orders as promptly as possible, chasing up customers where appropriate. Regular customers could be persuaded to buy in bulk rather than more frequently in smaller quantities. If orders require credit approval, salesmen should refer them immediately to the credit checking staff.

Credit Approvals

For orders above a certain size, credit should be granted with care. The credit of every substantial customer should be analyzed

- for any individual large order, or
- for the total amount of credit on the account.

The method of credit checking will vary according to the value of the order. Methods range from letters of reference from the customer's bank and from one or two other suppliers to the same customer, to an analysis of the customer's financial accounts. In addition, credit can be checked through credit reference agencies such as Equifax.

An objective of the system for credit approvals should be to limit credit risk from bad debts to an acceptable level. The scope for speeding up the credit approval process is limited by the requirement to control credit risk. The review will consider customer credit limits and procedures and criteria for accepting or rejecting credit requests. These should not be relaxed to the point where bad debts mount and become too costly.

However, the system should not be unnecessarily slow. The speed of the process should be continually reviewed. Where possible, telephone confirmation of credit should be given. Requests for credit approval should be handled promptly, and delays waiting for letters of reference or credit reports could be reduced by chasing up any that appear overdue. If the company uses its own credit records, these should be readily accessible on a database.

A review also could consider the minimum size of order requiring credit approval. If bad debts are low, the limit could be raised, and more orders processed without the need for approval.

Credit Terms

There are often accepted industry norms for credit terms, and it will be difficult for any company to insist on stricter terms for its own customers. Credit terms of 30 days net are common in many industries. This requires payment in full and with no discount within 30 days of the invoice date. In highly competitive industries, credit terms are more likely to be 60 days net or even 90 days net.

Terms also can vary according to the economic climate. In the downturn of the early 1990s, suppliers in many industries were prepared to allow customers a longer time to pay in order to win or keep their business.

It is important that the terms of payment should be made clear to the customer from the beginning. This can be done by printing the credit terms clearly on the invoice. For larger orders the company could insist on a deposit of perhaps 10% with the order.

Much selling between companies in EU countries is on open account and many clients charge interest on outstanding balances. Goods are supplied, the customer receives agreed credit terms and pays by an agreed method. The initiation of the payment comes from the customer.

Custom and practice varies from country to country and companies exporting to the EU should be aware of the payment times that might be expected. While this situation is likely to become increasingly standardized following the introduction of the euro, some differences between countries will still remain. In France, for example, normal credit terms for corporate customers can range up to 90 days or more, depending on the industrial sector. In Italy, by contrast, formal credit terms are commonly 30 days or less, but in practice, many companies take extensive credit beyond the permitted period.

Settlement discounts for early payment can be offered, but the interest costs of allowing these should not exceed the interest benefits from early payment, unless the company desperately needs the cash.

The approximate cost of an early settlement discount can be measured by the formula:

$$\left[\frac{D}{(100-D)}\times\frac{365}{(N-S)}\right]\%$$

where D is the discount offered (5% = 5, etc.)
N is the number of days credit offered net, for no discount
S is the number of days credit allowed with the settlement discount.

Example
Gamma grants credit terms of 60 days net to customers, but offers an early settlement discount of 2% for payment within seven days.

Analysis
Gamma is offering customers the option of paying \$98 after seven days per \$100 invoiced, or payment in full after 60 days. The approximate cost of the discount to Gamma is as follows:

$$\left[\frac{2}{(100-2)}\times\frac{365}{(60-7)}\right]\% = 14.1\%$$

The discount is only worthwhile financially if Gamma can save interest costs of 14.1% per annum or more, so that by obtaining $98 on day seven instead of $100 on day 60, more than $2 in interest costs could be saved in the time between day seven and day 60.

Where settlement discounts are offered, customers are likely to consider the financial benefits to themselves of paying in full after the allowed credit term or paying a smaller amount but earlier, by taking the settlement account. To make a discount attractive to customers, the interest benefit will have to be quite high, certainly higher than the interest rate available to the customer for keeping his cash on short-term deposit.

Dispatch

Three separate features of dispatch can create delays in cash collection.

- The speed of dispatch. Invoices normally cannot be sent out until the goods have been delivered.
- The turnaround of acknowledgements of receipt. If invoicing is dependent on the signing of a delivery note or other documentation by the customer, it is important to get the signed documentation to the invoicing staff as quickly as possible.
- Accuracy. Errors in the delivery itself, or in the documentation with the delivery, will cause hold-ups. The customer won't pay until he is satisfied. This could be a very serious problem when warehousing is inefficiently managed.

Inventory Control

Delays can arise because there is no stock available to meet an incoming order. Stock-outs of raw material hold up production, and stock-outs of finished goods can hold up dispatch and delivery to customers. When deliveries to customers are held up, there could be a knock-on effect, with confusion about invoicing. Invoices must be held up until delivery takes place, and without efficient procedures there is the likelihood that the invoice won't go out as soon as delivery eventually takes place. It is even conceivable that delayed invoices might be forgotten entirely.

In a review of inventory control, a company should check the frequency of unfulfilled orders and orders delayed by unavailable stock. A high incidence of delay should indicate scope for significant reductions in the collection cycle.

Invoicing

Invoicing methods and procedures should aim to ensure the prompt issue of customer invoices. A review of invoicing should include a check on the time between dispatch (as shown on the dispatch note or completion note signed by the customer) and the invoice date. If the delay seems excessive, the causes should be investigated.

Delays can occur because of slow invoicing procedures. For example, sending out an invoice might be held up until the accounts department receives the dispatch note that must be first matched up with a copy of the sales order form. Paperwork can build up and invoices could be processed at irregular intervals. The failure to produce invoices by computer also can waste valuable time. Invoices could be sent to the wrong part of the customer's organization, or to the wrong address. And there could be errors in invoice details.

If the invoice must be accompanied by other documentation, this needs to be complete and accurate. Errors will result in late payment or perhaps, in the case of export sales with letters of credit as the payment method, no payment at all.

For companies selling abroad, it would be advisable to produce invoices in two languages, English for a US exporting company, and the language of the customer's business. Delays could occur simply because the customer has difficulty in understanding the invoice.

Example
The accounts department of a company will close its books regularly, and for a short time stop making entries into the accounts in its ledgers. The

purpose of closing the books is to give the accounts department an opportunity to report on the financial position of the company at the month-end, by extracting information from its accounts. If the accounts were continually updated with new transactions, the task of preparing financial reports would become administratively complex and consequently prone to error.

The frequency with which a company closes its books varies according to its financial reporting requirement. Some companies close their books just once a year, at the end of their annual accounting period. Others might close their books twice a year, once every quarter or once a month.

The time during which the books remain closed also varies, but it can be several days. For example, a company with an accounting year ending on December 31, with very few business transactions at the year-end, might close its books around December 20 and not reopen them until the new year, on January 2. More commonly, closing the books could last two or three days.

When the books are closed, transactions are not recorded in the company's accounts. The company also will try to avoid having to make any payments during the period. In a well-managed business, however, the day-to-day routines of invoicing customers and collecting payments should not be affected. Invoices should be sent out promptly, and payments by customers should be banked as soon as possible. Accounting for invoices sent out and payments received can be done later, when the company's books are reopened.

It should be expected that most companies adopt this practice. However, there have been reported instances where the routine invoicing of customers has been held up for a few days because the company's books have been closed. If this were a regular monthly occurrence, a large number of customers would be invoiced later than necessary, and would therefore pay later, taking the full period from the invoice date allowed by its credit terms.

Debtor Control: Chasing Late Payments

If all customers paid in full and on time, there should be no problems at the payments stage of the collection cycle. However, in practice many customers don't pay on time, and debtor control systems are essential. The aims of debtor control should be to

- know who owes how much, and when payment is due
- know whose payments are overdue, by how much, and whether they have other debts in the pipeline or have placed other orders for future delivery
- handle queries from customers about invoices as quickly and efficiently as possible
- chase up late payers.

Regular reports should be prepared for payments outstanding. At an operational level, an aged debtors' list can itemize every overdue payment, and staff responsible for collections can chase up the customer. An aged debtors' list refers to unpaid amounts from customers in chronological order. At a management level there could be a regular report of days' sales outstanding, to allow management to monitor the customer payments situation.

A report on days' sales outstanding could give a figure for the average number of days from the invoice date before payment is actually received. The analysis could be broken down into days' sales outstanding for different groups of customers.

The company's information systems should pick up and record data about invoice and payment date so that a report can be prepared. Alternatively, a less accurate measurement of average debtor days can be obtained by the ratio

$$\text{Debtor days} = \frac{\text{Annual sales}}{\text{Average debtors}} \times 365$$

There should be a regular review of the number of customer complaints and queries, and the speed with which they are dealt. Conceivably, large amounts of unpaid debts could be the result of a slow response to customer queries.

The system for chasing up late payers should be reviewed carefully. The danger is that by pressing too hard for payment, a company can lose the long-term business of a good customer. Late payments could be preferable to losing business. It is equally important to take care with the credit approval process, to ensure that bad money is not thrown after good by continuing to supply a terminally ill company.

The ultimate threat to a late payer is court action, and guidelines ought to be established for the number and frequency of reminder/warning letters, and what action to take against non-payers. The key questions to consider are

- what should be the minimum value of an invoice to justify court action?
- When should court action be instigated?
- What procedures should be taken to ensure that the customer is given no further credit?

Payments Cycle Time

The payments cycle is similar to the cash collection cycle, and contains six elements.

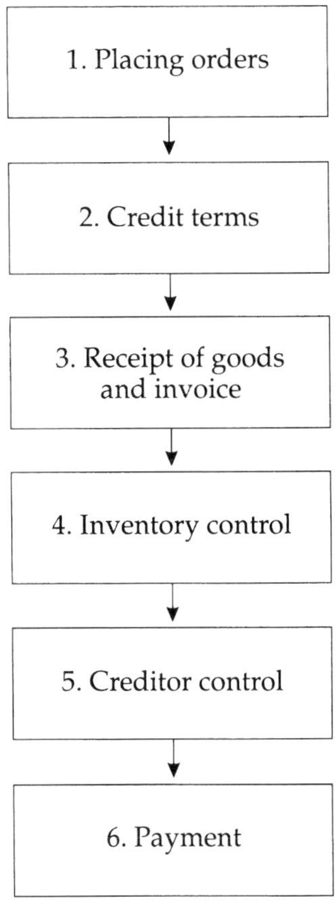

The payments cycle should be reviewed regularly to ensure that it is neither too short nor too long. It is costly to pay too early, but potentially damaging to supplier relationships to pay late.

Placing Orders. Credit Terms

Credit and credit terms should be agreed with the supplier, either in advance or when the order is placed. Credit terms are likely to be the industry norm, but there could be scope for negotiation.

- Large companies can often extract more favorable credit terms from small suppliers.
- Part of the negotiation could involve a trade-off between the length of credit allowed and a lower price. If the supplier offers a discount for early settlement, the benefits should exceed the interest cost of paying early.

If suppliers are offered a secure payment system, or a value-dated payment, they might be willing to give longer credit.

Receipt of Goods and Invoice. Inventory Control

There should be efficient procedures for receiving goods, and for processing the invoice and any supporting documentation. Goods received, the advice note, and the invoice should be checked against the order. Queries should be chased up promptly with the supplier. Payment should not be approved until any such queries have been answered satisfactorily.

Routine checks on inventories of purchased items should be made to identify slow-moving items that possibly are being purchased in excessive quantities, so that future purchases of the item could be delayed or reduced.

Creditor Control. Payment

A company should get to know its creditors. In some companies there are regular supplier reviews, analyzing which suppliers press for prompt payment and which allow credit in excess of the stipulated terms. The speed of payment to suppliers is then adjusted according to the findings in this analysis.

Payments should not be made early, except as an occasional favor to the supplier, and full use should be taken of the credit period that has been granted. Checks should be made from time to time to make sure that in practice payments are made at the intended time, and not before.

Commercial Consequences of Delayed Payments

A company should consider carefully the possible consequences of delaying payment to their suppliers. Delaying payment until the latest possible date benefits the paying company's cash flow at the expense of the supplying company, in effect transferring the cash problem to the supplier.

This can create or exacerbate funding problems for the supplier and even can result in the supplier going out of business. A company should consider the financial position and commercial importance of a supplier carefully before delaying any large payment. Such delaying action can sour a relationship and lead to a lower-quality service or even a cessation of business from the supplier.

The Japanese approach that involves regarding the supplier as a partner in the value chain, is clearly incompatible with an overly aggressive supplier payment policy.

Another possible consequence is the loss of potentially lucrative supplier discounts. Delaying payment until the final demand could be expensive in circumstances where discounts for early payment are available. For example, a 2% discount for payment within 30 days or non-discounted payment within 60 days, represents an effective investment return of 24%, far more than could be earned by delaying payment and investing the money in the money markets during the interim 30 days.

Some very large companies may feel that payments can be delayed so long as possible, well beyond the payment terms in a purchase contract, because the supplier is a small company and not in a position to complain without the risk of losing future business. Although effective in reducing the cash flow cycle time, this is a high-risk policy.

Summary

When a company has established its methods and procedures for cash collections and cash payments, they should be kept under review. This can be done by regular monitoring of the cash flow cycle. If the cycle is getting significantly longer, the reasons should be investigated.

The length of each part of the cycle – stock turnover, debt collection, and payments to suppliers – will vary from company to company and also according to the nature of the business and its products.

6

Control and Performance Reports

An objective of cash flow control is to achieve net cash flows or cash balances that satisfy a target or budget that management has set. The cash flow target could be to avoid borrowing, or to keep the amount borrowed within a specified overdraft limit. Targets could be imposed on a company by a bank, insisting that existing borrowing limits should not be breached and that interest payment obligations must be honored.

Control can be exercised in a number of ways; for example by cutting costs, delaying payments to suppliers, reducing stock levels or deferring capital expenditures. To apply control management needs information about cash flow performance.

Cash Flow Control Reports

Cash flow control reports should be prepared regularly for managers with responsibility for cash receipts, payments and balances. In many companies, reports could be restricted to the treasury department or financial controller's department. Reporting can be informal, perhaps a daily check on cleared funds in the company's bank accounts. Information about cleared balances can be obtained by telephone from the bank, or by calling up balance information via a PC modem link to an on-line banking system. The treasurer or financial controller can then judge whether the cash position is satisfactory, and cash in hand or borrowing facilities are sufficient to meet anticipated spending.

Cash flow control reporting can be more formal, with regular reports comparing the actual cash position against a target or budget. Reports can be distributed more widely, to operational managers as well as to treasurers and financial controllers. Widespread reporting of cash flows will be useful only if operational managers are conscious of a responsibility to control their cash flows as well as their costs and profits.

Operational Cash Flow Control Reports

Control reports could be prepared for operational cash flows that are the cash receipts and payments occurring in the day-to-day operations of a business. The frequency, format and structure of a control report can be designed to suit management requirements, but the purpose of the report should be to compare either

- actual cash flows against a budget or target, or
- a current forecast of cash flows against an original budget or target.

Example

A monthly cash flow control report, comparing actual and budget, is illustrated overleaf. Also illustrated is a half-yearly report, comparing a revised forecast of cash flows against the original budget.

Cash Flow Control Report

Alpha Language Schools: US Division
Month: March
Currency: dollars ($000s)

	Month Budget	Actual	Difference	Cumulative: Year to date Budget	Actual	Difference
Cash Receipts						
Tuition	1,100	1,150	+50	2,900	2,900	+80
Books	70	25	–45	210	155	–55
Cassettes	340	355	+15	650	692	+42
Sale of fixed assets	0	24	+24	30	24	–6
Other income	15	7	–8	45	44	–1
	1,525	1,561	+36	3,835	3,815	+60
Cash Payments						
Staff costs: teaching	390	496	+106	1,000	1,270	+270
Staff costs: management	250	248	–2	650	624	–26
Book purchases	60	32	–28	155	81	–74
Materials printing	25	28	+3	65	62	–3
Origination	15	19	+4	40	35	–5
Commissions	60	61	+1	155	158	+3
Advertising	85	113	+28	210	275	+65
Marketing expenses	72	69	–3	185	170	–15
Travel and entertaining	216	235	+19	520	499	–21
Equipment	60	72	+12	150	144	–6
Establishment	150	146	–4	450	435	–15
Office expenses	42	37	–5	100	96	–4
Other payments	30	24	–6	75	72	–3
	1,455	1,580	+125	3,755	3,921	+166
Net cash flow	+70	–19	–89	+80	–26	–106
Opening cash balance	22	5		12	12	–
Closing cash balance	92	–14		92	–14	–106

Revised Cash Flow Report

Beta Manufacturing
Month of Revised Forecast: July
Period to December 31

	Annual Budget	Revised Annual Forecast	Difference	Comments
	$000	$000	$000	
Cash Receipts				
Domestic sales	6,700	6,100	–600	
Export sales	2,500	2,200	–300	
Fixed asset sales	100	80	–20	
Other income	50	40	–10	
	9,350	8,420	–930	
Cash Payments				
Materials	1,900	1,780	–120	
Production staff	2,200	2,100	–100	
Production expenses	500	450	–50	
Administration	600	580	–20	
Advertising	300	295	–5	
Marketing	520	525	+5	
Commissions	80	70	–10	
Sales staff	700	720	+20	
Establishment	1,000	1,050	+50	
Other expenses	800	740	–60	
	8,600	8,310	–290	
Net cash flow	+750	+110	–640	
Opening cash balance	125	125	–	
Closing cash balance	875	235	–640	

Analysis

Control reports are useful only if they trigger a management response when actual cash flows or revised estimates differ significantly from budget. Reports could be discussed at monthly management meetings or at board meetings, and managers asked to explain differences or variances that exceed a certain control limit, perhaps a percentage of the budgeted cash flow figure.

In the example, the managers responsible could be asked to explain the high payments for teaching costs in March ($496,000 or 27% above the budget amount) and advertising ($113,000 or 33% above budget). The financial controller or director might be asked to comment on the company's borrowing limits, and whether in the light of the overspend, these are now expected to be sufficient.

It could be argued that control reports for operational cash flows are unnecessary because operational managers are also responsible for profitability. They will receive regular performance reports comparing actual operational profits against budget. Many cash receipts and payments will differ from budget because sales are higher or lower than expected, and costs are higher or lower. If these differences are picked up in a profit-and-loss report, there should be no need to repeat them in a cash flow report.

Profits are not the same as cash flows, however. A cash flow report would exclude notional charges such as depreciation, and could include cash payments for capital expenditure, and cash received from disposing of fixed assets. A cash flow report also would reflect any changes in the company's cash flow cycle times, for which operational managers might be responsible. They would reflect, for example, slower stock turnover time – a longer time between paying for stock and selling it – and an increase in debtor days – a longer time between selling goods or services and receiving payment from customers.

Notional Interest on Cash Borrowings or Surpluses

The accountability of operational managers for their divisional cash flows can be built into profit-and-loss reports by

- charging the division for interest on cash it has borrowed for its account from the company's or group's central treasury department, or

- crediting the division with interest for cash surpluses that it has transferred from its account to the company's or the group's central treasury.

Providing for notional interest in this way is feasible only if each operating division, for example, a subsidiary company, has its own bank account, borrows from a central source when it has a cash shortage, and transfers any cash surpluses to the central source. Differences between budgeted and actual notional interest would arise if actual cash flows differed from budget, and operational management could be asked to explain the difference. This is illustrated in the following table.

Gamma Division: Profit Report
Month: September

	Budget	Actual
	$000	$000
Sales	600	620
Costs		
Materials	180	175
Labor	240	260
Expenses	60	65
	480	500
Profit before interest	120	120
Notional interest	2	–1
Net profit	122	119

Each company can judge for itself whether an operational cash flow reporting system would be of value to management. Reports could be of particular value for

- start-up businesses where there will be large cash outflows before revenues are earned, and net cash payments have to be kept within an overall financing limit, and
- large capital expenditure projects. If cash flows from a project can be identified, regular reports could compare actual cash flows with the budget. These would help management to monitor and control project expenditures.

Financing and Investment Cash Flow Reports

Control reports can be prepared for financing and investment items, such as capital expenditures, borrowing, loan repayments, cash raised from share issues, interest and dividends (paid or received) and taxation payments.

Treasury departments should monitor their company's or group's cash flows and control reports, comparing actual against budget for these items could be useful. The contents and format for these reports are discussed more fully in the next chapter.

Other Cash Flow Control Reports

Other cash-flow reports could be used by financial controllers and treasurers. A control report could be produced for bank account balances at the end of or during a period. Such a report could monitor whether the balances have been within policy limits set for liquidity (cash surplus and maximum overdraft limit), or whether there have been idle cash balances that should have been invested.

A borrowing facilities report could indicate whether, and with how much of a safety margin, borrowing will remain within the limits of existing bank facilities.

Working Capital and Performance Reports

The management of working capital can be monitored by charging operational managers with a notional interest cost, as a percentage rate on the amount of working capital employed. This could act as an incentive to reduce working capital requirements, and control the cash flow cycle more efficiently.

Example

Alpha is a division of the Omega Group, and operates as a profit center. For the year to December 31, Alpha achieved operating profits of $800,000 before management interest. A charge is made against Alpha's profits by head office for management interest. This is the cost of funding Alpha's working capital requirements, and is calculated by applying a marginal cost of borrowing to the value of Alpha's net current assets (stocks plus debtors minus short-term creditors). The average value of Alpha's working capital items during the year was as follows:

	$
Stock	600,000
Debtors	900,000
Short-term creditors	400,000

An interest rate of 10% is applied.

Analysis

Alpha's reported profit will be $800,000 less the management interest charge of 10% on net current assets of $1,100,000 ($600,000 + $900,000 - $400,000).

	$
Trading profit	800,000
Management interest (10% of $1.1 million)	110,000
Net profit	690,000

Alpha's management might decide that there could be some reduction in stocks and debtors. By reducing working capital from $1.1 million to $900,000, for example, Alpha's net profit would increase by $20,000 (10% of $200,000). If Omega Group were borrowing short term to fund its operations, there also would be a cash saving for the group as a whole, because the reduction in working capital of $200,000 would release cash into the business and reduce Omega's need to borrow.

Summary

Cash flow control is a responsibility often given to treasurers and financial controllers. Operational managers are held responsible for profits, and therefore cash flows might be given little or no attention in routine operational reports.

Companies should consider whether generating cash flow control reports yields tangible benefits. Alternatively, profit performance reports could give some recognition to cash flow management and working capital management by including notional interest within the profits of each reporting operational unit or division.

Cash Flow Statements

In many countries, including the US and the UK, larger companies, with some exceptions for wholly owned subsidiary companies, are required to present a cash flow statement as part of their published accounts. The amount of detail that must be disclosed in the cash flow statement differs between countries.

Purpose

The purpose of a cash flow statement is for the company to report, in a standard format, how it has generated and absorbed cash over the reporting period (usually 12 months). The statement includes details about operating, financing and investment cash flows, and is intended to provide information for assessing the company's liquidity, viability and financial flexibility.

Liquidity

If a company's balance sheet indicates a poor liquidity position, perhaps with a high bank overdraft, a cash flow statement should indicate what has been happening to the cash position, and why it is so bad or getting worse. When liquidity is high, the main sources of cash generation should be apparent from a cash flow statement.

Viability
A company must have good cash flows to survive, especially in the short term. Profitable companies have gone into liquidation or have had to sell off parts of their business operations because they did not generate enough cash. A cash flow statement should indicate whether a company is obtaining sufficient cash from its normal operations to remain viable, or whether it might be getting into difficulty.

Financial Flexibility
Financial flexibility lets a company choose what it wants to spend money on, and when. It comes from having sound cash flows and good liquidity. A company with positive operational cash flows and a large amount of surplus cash is in a good position to purchase new assets or businesses whenever the opportunity arises. Similarly, positive cash flows give a company greater flexibility when it comes to deciding how large a dividend it can afford to pay out to shareholders. Dividends could be restricted by poor liquidity.

What has happened to cash flows in the past can provide an excellent guide to what is likely to happen in the future, and this is a rationale for requiring companies to present a cash flow statement. A cash flow statement should be included as part of a company's annual report and accounts, where it may be used by individuals outside company management, in particular, users of published accounts such as shareholders and investment analysts.

The same information, perhaps produced quarterly or half-yearly and presented in the same format, also should be useful to senior management and company treasurers.

While this book is not intended to describe the accounting rules for cash flow statements in any great detail, it will be useful to consider

- the general structure of a cash flow statement and the information it contains
- how this information might be analyzed
- the implications for cash management of the requirement to publish cash flow information.

Format

A statement assembles cash flows under headings or categories that include

- Operating activities
- Returns on investments and servicing of finance
- Taxation
- Capital expenditure and financial investment
- Acquisitions and disposals
- Dividends paid
- Management of liquid resources
- Financing.

Taken together, these will determine an increase or a decrease in the company's cash balances during a defined period.

Example

Alpha Group: Cash Flow Statement for the Year Ended December 31
American Express Company

	1998 $000	1997 $000
Cash flow from operating activities		
Net income	2,141	1,991
Adjustments to reconcile net income to net cash provided by operating activities		
Provisions for losses and benefits	2,491	2,307
Depreciation, amortization, deferred taxes and others	(212)	187
Changes in operating assets and liabilities, net of effects of	(152)	
Acquisitions and dispositions:	(665)	(227)
Accounts receivable and accrued interest	92	334
Other assets	131	517
Accounts payable and other liabilities		

	1998	1997
	$000	$000
Increase (decrease) in travelers' cheques	253	(111)
outstanding	182	172
Increase in insurance reserves	–	–
FDC Gain	4,413	5,170
Net cash used by operating activities		
Cash Flows for Investing Activities		
Sale of investments	1,656	1,778
Maturity and redemption of investments	7,331	4,827
Purchase of investments	(10,176)	(7,898)
Net increase in receivables	(1,510)	(2,575)
Loans/receivables sold to Trust, net	1,683	516
Proceeds from repayment of loans	24,791	25,591
Issuance of loans	(27,587)	(29,304)
Purchase of land, buildings and equipment	(391)	(343)
Sale of land, buildings and equipment	26	164
(Acquisitions) dispositions, net of cash	(471)	23
acquired/sold	(4,648)	(7,221)
Net cash used by investing activities		
Cash Flows from Financing Activities		
Net increase (decrease) in customers' deposits	1,039	733
Sale of annuities and investment certificates	5,337	5,888
Redemption of annuities and investment certificates	(5,690)	(4,965)
Net increase in debt with maturities of 3 months	1,239	3,823
or less	7,373	11,439
Issuance of debt	(7,426)	(11,604)
Principal payments on debt	500	–
Issuance of Trust preferred securities		
Issuance of American Express common shares	137	168
Repurchase of American Express common shares	(1,890)	(1,259)
Dividends paid	(414)	(423)
Net cash provided (used) by financing activities	205	3,800
Effect of exchange rate changes on cash		
Net decrease (increase) in cash and cash equivalents	(87)	1,502
Cash and cash equivalents at beginning of year	4,179	2,677
Cash and cash equivalents at end of year	4,092	4,179

Operating Activities

Operating cash flows are the cash flows from trading operations. Every business should be trying to achieve healthy positive operational cash flows and this is a key item in the statement.

Cash flows from operating activities may be reported as just a single net figure at the beginning of the statement. Alternatively, the company could provide more information by reporting the gross amounts for

- cash received from customers
- cash payments to suppliers
- cash paid to and on behalf of employees
- other cash pay.

Analysis
Operating income and net cash from operations are not the same amount, mainly for three reasons

- depreciation
- profits or losses on fixed asset sales
- working capital changes.

Depreciation is a charge against profits that allocates a cost to the period for the use of fixed assets. It is a notional or paper cost, and does not represent a cash flow. Net cash inflows therefore should be higher than operating income by the amount of the depreciation charge.

When a company disposes of fixed assets, it reports a profit or loss on the sale. This is the difference between the sale price obtained and the value at the time of sale of the fixed asset in the company's accounting records. For example, if fixed assets that have a net book value of $38,000 in the accounts are sold for $50,000, there will be a profit on the sale of $12,000. Operating income will include this $12,000. The cash value of the sale, however, is $50,000, not $12,000. In a cash flow statement, income on fixed asset sales is therefore deducted from the operating income figure because it is not a cash receipt. Losses on fixed asset sales would be added.

The effect on cash flows of changes in working capital (stocks, debtors and creditors) has been explained in Chapter 4 on the cash flow cycle. When there is an increase in stocks and debtors, or a decrease in creditors, cash inflows will be lower than operating income. A reduction in stocks and debtors, as an increase in creditors, will result in cash inflows higher than the operating income. For example, if a company makes an operating income of $500,000, but has an increase in stock and debtors of $23,000, the cash received from operations will be $23,000 lower than the operating income.

Returns on Investments and Servicing of Finance

The cash flow statement shows receipts and payments of interest and dividends received. Equity dividend payments are shown under a separate heading before Financing.

Taxation

The cash flow statement also takes into account tax on income. Income taxes affect a firm's profitability and its cash flows. Deferred tax assets and deferred tax liabilities also affect cash flows. The underlying concept here is matching: matching income tax expense with the income reported for financial reporting, even though the associated cash flows for income taxes will not occure until future periods.

Capital Expenditure

This consists principally of cash payments for purchase of fixed assets and cash income from the sale of fixed assets.

Acquisitions and Disposals

The main cash flows will comprise purchase and sale of business divisions and companies. The purchase of a subsidiary could be paid for partly in cash and partly by issuing shares or loan stock. A cash flow statement must give information about what has been purchased, and how much of the purchase price has been paid in cash.

Example

Purchase of subsidiary

	$000
Net assets acquired	
Tangible fixed assets	200
Stocks	60
Debtors	50
Cash at bank and in hand	25
Creditors	(20)
Bank facilities	(10)
Proposed dividend	(10)
Loans	(90)
Goodwill	325
	530
Satisfied by	
Shares allotted	400
Cash	130
	530

Analysis of the net inflow of cash and cash equivalents in respect of the purchase of the subsidiary undertaking

	$000
Cash consideration	130
Cash at bank and in hand acquired	(25)
Bank facilities of acquired subsidiary	10
Net cash used and cash equivalents in respect of the purchase	115

Analysis

These two tables taken together explain the cash payment for acquiring the subsidiary. In this example, the subsidiary was purchased for $530,000, of which $400,000 was paid by issuing shares to the seller and $130,000 in cash. The company acquired the subsidiary's cash of $25,000 and its loan of $10,000, so that the net cash payment was $115,000 ($130,000 minus the $15,000 of net cash acquired).

Sale of a Business

A similar analysis would be shown for the sale of businesses as for the purchase of subsidiaries.

Equity Dividends Paid

Cash flow payments for dividends will consist of the previous year's final dividend, to which the company commits itself at the shareholders' annual general meeting, plus the current year's interim dividend.

Financing Activities

A cash flow statement shows the net cash flows from operating activities, interest, dividends, tax and investing activities.

- If there is a net cash inflow, the company either must have reduced its borrowings or increased its holding of cash.
- If there is a net cash outflow, the company must either have raised extra funds or suffered a fall in its cash balances.

Financing cash flows are associated with the external funding of the business. They consist primarily of

- cash inflows from issuing shares, debentures, loan stock, notes, bonds, etc
- cash inflows from new loans, excluding changes in the bank overdraft
- cash repayments of loan principal
- cash expenses associated with the issue of shares or bonds, or with raising loans.

Management of Liquid Resources

Liquid resources are defined by the standard as readily disposable stores of value that are

- disposed by the reporting entity without curtailing or disrupting its business and are either

- readily convertible into known amounts of cash at or close to their carrying amount
- or are traded in an active market.

Cash inflows in management of liquid resources include

- withdrawals from short-term deposits
- inflows from disposal or redemption of any other investments held as liquid resources.

Cash outflows in management of liquid resources include

- payments into short-term deposits
- outflows to acquire any other investments that are held as liquid resources.

Each entity should explain what it includes as liquid resources and any changes in its policy.

Footnotes to the Statement

Cash flow statements must be accompanied by several footnotes giving further details to make the statement more comprehensible, and to help those reading it understand how cash flows relate to profits and changes in the company's balance sheet position since the previous year.

Interpreting Cash Flow Statements

Cash-flow problems do not happen overnight. They build up over time, and analysis of historical cash flows and trends over the past year or two can be very instructive.

The analysis can begin with the company's ability to generate cash from profits and then assess wider issues of cash management. In particular, key questions are

- How much cash is the company generating from its operations?

- Is this enough for the company's needs?
- Is it possible to make estimates or projections of the company's cash flows in the future, in order to assess liquidity and creditworthiness?

The format of the cash flow statement helps users to make a broad distinction between

- operating cash flow
- cash flows for essential spending such as interest payments and taxation (priority cash flows)
- discretionary cash flows, capital expenditure, etc.
- financing cash flow.

A concept sometimes used in financial analysis is *free cash flow*. This is the surplus cash available from operating activities, after paying for essential items such as interest and taxation. Free cash flow can be equated with the net amount of cash flows from operating activities, returns on investments and servicing of finance, and taxation.

It is then possible to judge the extent to which investment spending has been financed out of free cash flow, and how much has been financed by raising new money from external sources. Similarly, the ability of a company to make forthcoming repayments of loan principal out of free cash flow could be estimated from a study of its historical cash flows, with free cash flow again a key item for analysis.

Cash Flow Ratios

An analysis of cash flow statements can be attempted by calculating and comparing various ratios. It is useful, for example, to compare the relative size of the net inflow from operational activities with other items of cash flow.

Operational Cash Flow and Priority Cash Flows

The ratio of operational cash flow to priority cash outflows, sometimes referred to as the debt service ratio, measures the ability of a company to pay its priority outflows from operational cash flows.

$$\frac{\text{Operational cash flows}}{\text{Priority cash outflows}}$$

Monitoring the trend of this ratio over time would suggest whether the company's cash-generative abilities are improving or deteriorating. A very low ratio would suggest an inability, without further long-term funding, to pay dividends and to make essential capital investments.

Internal Financing Ratio

Capital expenditure (capex) is an important element in the cash flows of many companies. It could be regarded as a discretionary cash flow item, but in reality fixed asset replacement can be essential if a company is to survive in the long term.

Fixed assets must be replaced eventually. It is helpful to judge what minimum level of capex seems necessary for the business, and how much of the discretionary outflows are really more essential than optional.

Price inflation will mean that the cost of replacing fixed assets normally will exceed the original cost of the old assets, and it is not contentious to suggest that annual capital expenditure, as a minimum requirement, should normally be higher than the depreciation charge in the profit and loss account.

It is reasonable to expect that in the long term, but not necessarily year by year, a company should be able to finance most of its capital expenditures from its own operational cash flows, with just a small proportion financed by new borrowing, even allowing for dividend payments to stockholders.

In other words in the long-term, operational cash flows, minus priority cash flows and dividend payments, should be about the same amount as capital expenditure outflows. A company should be able to finance most of its capital expenditures internally.

A suitable ratio for measuring a company's performance on this issue is the internal financing ratio.

Capital expenditure payments should include payments for acquisitions but exclude payments to acquire investments, for example purchase of money market investments. Priority cash flows should include dividends paid. The internal financing ratio might be greater than or less than one in any particular year, but in the long term, it ought to be fairly close to one on average. If it is greater than one, the company will be using new borrowing to finance some of its capital expenditure program. Just how much capital expenditure is being financed by borrowing obviously is significant to an assessment of the company's cash-generative capability.

Implications of Cash Flow Statements

The requirement for larger companies to publish cash flow statements has important implications for company management. Cash flow statements could be regarded as incidental to liquidity management, because they are for external reporting to stockholders and analysts, rather than for internal reporting to management. However, the greater prominence given to cash flow in financial reporting could have repercussions on the control systems by which management plans its cash flows, sets cash targets and monitors cash flow performance.

Cash Management Audit

Control reports and cash flow statements, while providing information about a company's cash flows, do not consider the efficiency of the organization and systems for cash flow management. However, companies should review their systems from time to time. One way of doing this is to carry out a cash management audit. Audit is simply a term for a thorough and systematic investigation of the systems and controls for cash management. The purpose of an audit should be to consider whether the cash management system is efficient and whether it is suitable for current conditions. As in other areas of business, conditions and circumstances change over time. A cash management system that was appropriate several years ago might not be as efficient as the most up-to-date system.

The increasing automation of banking services, new systems for cross-border cash management and new banking regulations can act as a catalyst for change in a company's cash management system. The systems of many large multinational companies have become very sophisticated, and there is every reason to suppose that changes and developments will continue in the future.

Influences for Change

Changes in cash management systems in recent years have been prompted by several factors, including

- volatile interest rates
- volatile exchange rates

- deregulation of the financial markets
- new banking technology
- business reorganization.

Volatile Interest Rates

Interest rates have fluctuated widely over relatively short periods.

During the recession of the early 1990s banks compensated for the risk of greater bad debts by setting interest rates on lending at a higher premium above base rate or LIBOR, especially for smaller customers. Capital-adequacy-ratio requirements are forcing banks to look more carefully at their lending activities, and it is probable that interest rates to customers will remain higher in real terms than they did in the past. High real interest rates are a deterrent to borrowing and an incentive to better cash management.

Volatile Exchange Rates

For companies that have income and expenditure in several currencies, large swings in exchange rates have created serious exposures to currency risk. The dollar, for example, has been particularly volatile during the past ten years. For example, in 1989 the $/DM rate was around 1.95. By late 1992, the dollar had dropped to 1.4, rallying to 1.75 in 1993 and sliding back down to 1.4 by March 1995. However, by late 1998 there had been a gradual stabilization to 1.8.

The dollar is the major currency for international trade and its changing value over time relative to other currencies, has created problems for companies, particularly those operating on narrow profit margins in international markets such as electronic goods. Efficient cash management can help these companies to reduce their exposures to currency risk. Implementation of the euro is expected to moderate intra-European currency rate fluctuations with respect to the dollar and it is very possible that the euro may find itself an increasingly strong reference currency vis à vis the dollar.

Deregulation of the Financial Markets

The financial markets in many countries have gone or are going through a period of deregulation. Lending and money transfer arrangements are less restrictive than in the past, and banking systems have been expanding their capabilities. The scope for further deregulation is still large.

New Banking Technology

Advanced information technology systems have developed in step with the changing demands of corporate customers. There also has been a more widespread use of long-established systems. Cash budgets, for example, are now commonly prepared with spreadsheet programs on a fairly inexpensive PC, extracting key financial data directly from mainframe units where they can be manipulated for forecasting purposes on an Excel spreadsheet. Electronic banking systems have been adopted more widely because their cost has come down, allowing smaller companies to justify their cost. These offer a variety of facilities for monitoring outstanding balances and for managing money transfers.

Business Reorganizations

Internal changes within a company, such as a merger or acquisition, or the rationalization of business units, can result in a restructuring of the cash management function. A trend towards centralization of operations, particularly by multinationals in Europe also can be expected. Several central treasury departments in large multinationals have been reestablished to act as a central bank or finance company for the rest of the group. Each operating division deals with the central treasury as its bank for such functions as lending, hedging currency risks and interest rate risks. The treasury department then has sole responsibility for dealing with external banks for the group's cash and risk management requirements.

Identifying the Need for an Audit

A cash management or treasury audit, is a review of an organization's existing systems with a view to identifying inefficiencies and proposing improvements. Given the pace of change in banking systems and company organization structures, a regular audit isdesirable. There are a number of events or conditions, however, that might prompt management to set an investigation in motion. Some of these are listed.

- The company has an increasing number of locations at which cash is paid out or received.
- The volume and value of cash transactions is increasing.
- The company has been opening new bank accounts and now may have too many.
- A bank has recommended an improved electronic banking system, or has indicated that a new system will soon become available.
- The company is undergoing a major reorganization.
- Unauthorized cash transactions or other financial transactions have been uncovered, suggesting inadequate controls.
- The company's need for working capital is increasing at a faster rate than business growth would justify, or is not declining despite a drop in business volume. Deterioration in accounts receivable, that is the time taken by credit customers to pay, might be the cause.
- The company does not have written policies or procedures for its cash and treasury management operations. Alternatively, written procedures may exist but they have not been reviewed and updated for some time.

Example
A multinational company has a subsidiary in Switzerland. The company has a Swiss franc account with its bank in New York. The Swiss subsidiary deals with most of its operational payments and receipts, and transfers surplus funds to the New York account monthly. For high-value sales, however, the New York head office invoices customers directly in Swiss francs. A cash management audit shows that in the absence of

exchange controls between countries in which the company operates, suitable electronic systems are available to transfer funds quickly across national borders. The audit team recommends that the company relocates its main Swiss franc account with a bank in Switzerland, and give the local subsidiary responsibility for invoicing all receivables, regardless of size. The expected benefit is a quicker collection of amounts due and lower banking costs. The transaction charge for a payment by a Swiss customer into an account in Switzerland is less than for a payment into a Swiss franc account in New York. At the same time, all receipts in Swiss francs from anywhere in the group could be transferred to the Swiss account that also would be used for all payments in Swiss francs by companies in the group.

Establishing an Audit

A company could establish its own in-house audit team, appoint an external consultant, or use a mixture of both. External consultants have the advantages of specialization and experience in fact-finding and analysis, as well as familiarity with alternative systems that might be established. With in-house staff there are the advantages of a thorough knowledge of their company's businesses and a permanent presence. Consultants stay for the term of their appointment and no longer, but can work fulltime on the project. In-house staff, by contrast, can carry out an ongoing and so more thorough audit. However, it might be difficult to assign staff to the project and away from their other work for more than just a few weeks.

Stages in the Audit Process

The broad stages of a cash management audit are

- fact-finding
- analysis and identification of weaknesses
- developing proposals for improvement
- evaluating the benefits and estimating the costs of each

proposal
- recommending improvements
- implementation.

Fact-finding

The purpose of fact-finding is quite simply to establish what cash management systems are in operation, what the cash flows and average cash balances of the organization are, where they are held, and how quickly cash is collected. The audit should cover the areas of cash planning and budgeting, and budgeting control, as well as all the cash handling systems.

The process of fact-finding should use a suitable mix of site visits and questionnaires. Site visits are time consuming and might be restricted in number. However, they allow the investigator to carry out an in-depth analysis and obtain better-quality data from face-to-face questioning and seeing the system in operation.

Questionnaires, on the other hand, can be sent out to larger numbers of people. Unlike site visits, they should not disrupt workflow because they can be completed at convenient moments, even over a period of several days if necessary.

Large organizations might opt for a small number of site visits and more widespread use of audit questionnaires. A danger with any type of fact-finding is that the data collected could be incorrect or incomplete. The audit team could misunderstand the information they are given, or overlook some important details. It is therefore advisable to get the data checked and verified by operational management before proceeding to the next stage of the audit.

Analysis

The information gathered from site visits and questionnaires should be analyzed, and potential weaknesses and inefficiencies identified. The key areas for analysis are cash receipts (receivables) and payments (payables), bank balances and bank charges. The analysis should concentrate on the rationale for all the cash movements and their timing.

Cash Receivables

For cash receivables, the audit should focus on the receivables float, i.e. the time from making a sale to the time of receipt of the cash payment from the customer. In companies that conduct regular audits, the audit team could compare the current float time with previous years, in order to assess improvement or deterioration. Items for review should include

- the time from sale to creating an invoice, and whether unnecessary delays occur
- the frequency of customer queries about invoice details, or incorrect payments because of an unclear or badly designed order form or invoice
- credit terms offered to customers
- promptness of payments by customers
- the proportion of customers whose late payments must be chased up
- the promptness with which late payers are contacted to chase up overdue payment
- the use of early settlement discounts and the number of customers taking advantage of them
- procedures for banking money received
- invoice dating. If customers are asked to pay within a stated number of days of the invoice date, invoices should be dated, and clearly state the credit terms.

Cash Payables

A major potential weakness with cash payables is paying invoices before the due date. Another weakness could be costly decisions about early-settlement discounts – taking discounts for which the terms are not beneficial, or refusing to accept discounts on favorable terms.

It might be argued that delaying payments to suppliers beyond the due date is good cash management practice. However, such a policy could damage supplier relationships, and make suppliers less willing to extend further credit to the company.

Bank Balances and Bank Charges
Bank charges should be checked for accuracy. Charges can vary between banks, and banks occasionally make mistakes.

In order to meet the concerns of many businesses, a number of off-the-shelf software packages have been developed that monitor and check bank interest and charges and how they can be calculated.

Companies that receive large amounts by direct debit should check on how prompt their bank is in collecting payments. Delays sometimes occur, costing the company extra in overdraft charges or loss of earnings on deposit.

The use of cash balances should be reviewed, including the interest yields receivable from cash on deposit. The audit might also consider the time taken by banks to provide cleared funds after receipts from customers have been banked.

Recommending Improvements

Having identified weaknesses in the existing system, the cash management audit team should develop proposals for change. The benefits of change can be large. By reducing the average time to collect debts by just one day, a company with an annual turnover of $40 million, for example, could save almost $11,000 per annum when interest rates were at 10%.

Alternative arrangements could be considered; for example, pooling, netting and reinvoicing arrangements, different methods of payment, or the use of foreign currency bank accounts or bank accounts in other countries. Each proposal should be documented and costed, and the expected benefits evaluated. A cash flow map could be drawn, showing what the cash flows would have been if these alternative arrangements had been applied. If the alternative arrangements seem superior to those currently in use, a plan could be formulated for changing over to them.

Arrangements could be planned in consultation with the company's existing bank, but it might be necessary to approach other banks that have the appropriate technology, software or location. Although the new arrangements would be initiated by head office, consultation with local business units would be necessary to obtain their agreement.

Recommended proposals would then be submitted in a report to the board for approval. It might be appropriate to include in the report any proposals that were considered but rejected as being unworkable or too costly for the benefits obtainable.

Summary

A cash management audit is simply a formal investigation into a company's cash management systems, to identify weaknesses and areas for change or improvement. It is not intended to find fault with what managers are doing. Developments within a company, such as an increase or reduction in its size, or in banking technology, could mean that existing cash-management systems are no longer the best in the current circumstances. An audit should identify if and when this has occurred. Regular audit investigations help to make sure that cash management systems are reviewed. They also promote a culture of cash-consciousness within the company.

Introducing a More Efficient Cash Management System

Precondition: resource the cash management function with able financial manager(s).

Quantify business cash flows	Identify the size of all cash flows into and out of the business. Identify the direction of such flows. Determine the reasons for such flows, their commercial validity and the extent to which they are time critical.
Create an optimal cash flow map	Reassess the rationale for and timing of cash flows. Identify improvements to reduce cash flow volatility and to take advantage of netting, tax and other considerations. Document the revised cash flow arrangements as a map of inflows, outflows and transfers.
Plan the implementation of this optimal cash flow map	Assess commercial banking needs in the light of existing bank relationships. Determine the credit appetite and technological capability of target banks. Define mechanisms for cash flow control.
Obtain consensus agreement of business units to the cash flow map, at working and senior management level	
Obtain board approval	
Document cash management policies and procedures	
Tactical implementation	Negotiate with banks. Educate staff of the organization. Allocate cash flow responsibilities to nominated staff. If possible, test the new system, operating it in parallel for a time with the previous system. Identify flaws and amend as needed.
Review the efficiency of the system regularly	Challenge the need for every cash flow item, existing or new.

Conclusion

Cash flow control is concerned with ensuring the viability, liquidity, and financial flexibility of a business organization. In large companies, the problems of control are more acute because responsibilities are shared between more people and between business units. For multinationals, there are the added complexities of tax and banking regulations and currency risk.

Controls rely on effective organization, planning, and a regular supply of information to management. Plans can vary in type, from policy guidelines to budgets and procedural rules. Control consists largely of ensuring that policies are carried out, budgets achieved, and rules obeyed. Control reports should be prepared for management, indicating whether cash flow planning targets are being met. Regular policy reviews and audits can establish whether systems are still adequate and that rules are properly applied.

A business must be profitable in the long term to generate cash from its operating activities, but cash flows can be improved by controlling the cash flow cycle. A shorter cash flow cycle will reduce the amount of funds tied up in working capital, but changing cash flow cycle times also has implications for liquidity.

Requiring large companies to include a cash flow statement in their annual accounts has resulted in a closer scrutiny of corporate cash flows than in the past. A particular concern for stock market analysts, and so for company directors, is the size of cash flows from ongoing operations rather than investment and financing cash flows.

Control is a continuous process. Plans are regularly formulated, applied, reviewed, and amended or updated. Controls are applied at all levels of management, from a supervisor's enforcement of rules and procedures to policy reviews at board level. Regular checks on internal controls can establish whether the system should be altered or updated.

Glossary

Acid Test Ratio

Ratio of liquid assets (current assets excluding stocks) to current liabilities. The acid test ratio is also called the quick ratio. See also Current Ratio.

Audit

A systematic examination involving the investigation and analysis of a system, including its procedures, etc., and its controls and its records.

Cash Equivalent

Term used in cash flow statements to mean time deposits and cash investments with up to three months to maturity from when they were acquired.

Cash Flow Cycle

The continuous process of paying out cash for operational expenditures and subsequently receiving cash from sales. This can be depicted as a cycle of cash out, cash in, cash out, cash in.

Cash Flow Cycle Time

A measurement of time between making payments for operational expenditures and receiving payment from customers. In a retail business, it is the time from paying suppliers to receiving payment for retail sales.

Currency Risk

Risk of losses, including lower income, higher costs, loss of asset values, etc., from an adverse movement in exchange rates.

Current Asset
Asset of a business held short term to support the trading cycle of the business. Current assets include stocks, debtors and cash.

Current Liability
Amount due for payment/settlement within one year.

Current Ratio
Ratio of liquid assets (current assets) to current liabilities. See also Acid Test Ratio.

Debt Service Ratio
A ratio of a company's operational cash flows to its commitments to pay interest, tax and other priority cash flows.

Debtor Days
Average time between making a sale and receipt of payment from the customer. Measured in days.

Electronic Banking System
Computerized system linking a customer via a terminal to his bank. A system can be used to obtain information about cash balances and transactions on the customer's account, and to send money transfer instructions to the bank.

Free Cash Flow
Operational cash flows left over for a business after having paid for priority cash flow items, and available for discretionary spending.

Internal Controls
Controls to ensure that functions are performed in an orderly and efficient way, that all assets are safeguarded, that records are both accurate and complete, and that management policies are being applied.

Internal Financing Ratio
Ratio of a company's capital expenditure payments to its free cash flow.

Liquidity
Having sufficient cash and near-cash, i.e. assets that soon will become cash, such as debtors, and assets that could be converted at short notice into cash, including money-market investments.

Mandate
A bank mandate is a document held by a customer's bank that lists the signatures of individuals authorized to sign checks and send payment instructions.

Management Accounts
Accounting records and information used by management for planning and controlling of the business.

Multinational Company
A company with business units, usually subsidiary companies, operating in more than one country.

Netting
Arrangement for simplifying and regulating payments between business units in a company or a group. Payments are reduced to a single money transfer for each business unit, in the form of a net amount receivable or a net amount payable. Net payments are made to or received from a netting center.

Notional Interest
An amount for interest (cost or income) used in management accounts for reporting divisional profits. A selected rate of interest is applied to the value of capital resources employed by the division, or to amounts of cash transferred to or from the division.

Offshore Company
Company registered in a different country. Offshore usually has the connotation of a company being registered in a particular country to benefit from its favorable local tax conditions and regulations.

Operational Cash Flows
Cash receipts and payments in the course of normal trading operations.

Overtrading
Over-reliance on short-term credit to finance business operations. Overtrading can be evident in rapidly growing businesses that delay payments to creditors and use a bank overdraft facility to its limit.

Pooling
Arrangement whereby cash balances on a number of bank accounts are transferred automatically, or at the discretion of management, into a central account or cash pool.

Priority Cash Flow
Cash flow that must be paid by a business to remain viable. Priority cash flows include taxation and interest payments.

Quick Ratio
See Acid Test Ratio.

Reinvoicing Center
Central finance company, often offshore, in a multinational group. Other subsidiaries sell goods to customers but send invoices to the reinvoicing center that issues its own invoices to customers. Similarly for purchases by group subsidiaries, suppliers' invoices are sent to the reinvoicing center that in turn issues its own invoices to the purchasing subsidiary.

Settlement Discount
Discount offered to customers for early payment of invoices.

Trading Cycle
The continuous cycle of buying and selling in business. A trading cycle is the time from purchasing resources to selling them, perhaps as part of a service or manufactured product.

Working Capital

The amount of funds needed to support day-to-day operations of a business. It consists of stocks and debtors, and possibly a minimum cash balance, minus short-term trade creditors. An alternative but similar definition of working capital is net current assets, i.e. the total current assets of a business minus its total current liabilities. Current liabilities are shown in a balance sheet as Creditors: amounts falling due in less than one year.

Index